MORE
AFRICAN
AMERICAN
Special Days

15 ADDITIONAL COMPLETE WORSHIP SERVICES

Cheryl A. Kirk-Duggan

ABINGDON PRESS
NASHVILLE

MORE AFRICAN AMERICAN SPECIAL DAYS
15 ADDITIONAL COMPLETE WORSHIP SERVICES

Copyright © 2005 by Cheryl A. Kirk-Duggan

This book is printed on acid-free paper.

Library of Congress Cataloging-in-Publication Data

Kirk-Duggan, Cheryl A.
    More African American special days : 15 additional complete worship services
/ Cheryl A. Kirk-Duggan.
        p. cm.
    ISBN 0-687-34364-X (alk. paper)
    1. African Americans—Religion. 2. Fasts and feasts. I. Title.

BR563.N4K575 2005
253'.97'08996073—dc22

                                                                2004019906

All scripture quotations are taken from the *New Revised Standard Version of the
Bible,* copyright © 1989, by the Division of Christian Education of the National
Council of the Churches of Christ in the United States of America. Used by per-
mission.

Illustrations by Ron Hester

05 06 07 08 09 10 11 12 13 14—10 9 8 7 6 5 4 3 2 1

MANUFACTURED IN THE UNITED STATES OF AMERICA

To
Jessie Katherine Wilson, "J.K."
Consumate Leader, Friend, Mother, Grandmother,
Great-grandmother

CONTENTS

ACKNOWLEDGMENTS

Throughout my years of development as a person, musician, minister, and professor, I have had the support and the engagement of the "souls of Black folk." I have served and been served by family and countless extended families in the guise of church families, pastors, Sunday school teachers, choir directors, and a wonderful host of laypeople, all of whom are the salt of the earth. They have loved and mentored me, challenged me and encouraged me; and they have helped me come to a place of excellence in all that I do, from my writing to my pastoral presence. For their care and commitment to my experience of God's call in my life, I am eternally grateful.

For my "cloud of witnesses" in all the congregations where I have served on staff or impromptu, I express my deepest thanks, including: Reeves Temple C.M.E. Church, Lake Charles, Louisiana; Trinity C.M.E., Lafayette, Louisiana; Williams Institutional C.M.E., New York, New York; Simpson United Methodist Church, Austin, Texas; Trinity C.M.E. Austin, Texas; Newman Center, Austin, Texas; Russell Memorial C.M.E. Church, Durham, North Carolina; Holy Cross Catholic Church, Durham, North Carolina; Phillips Temple C.M.E. Church, Berkeley, California; and St. Columba Catholic Church, Oakland, California. Thanks to all of my prayer partners, who have walked this part of my journey with me.

INTRODUCTION

Some people think of liturgical churches as those that strictly follow the liturgical calendar of the Christian year, including Advent, Epiphany, Lent, Easter, Pentecost, Ordinary time, and Kingdomtide, with particular colors, rituals, scriptures, and so forth. These churches include the Methodist, Roman Catholic, Orthodox, Episcopal, and Lutheran. There are many African Americans who belong to these mainline denominations. There are other churches that participate in liturgy without adhering strictly to the Christian year; some churches do a combination. Clearly, churches that have formal services have rituals and have devised liturgical drama that works for their understanding of church, scripture, and ministry.

African American Special Days has celebrated this liturgical drama since 1996. Many pastors and religious leaders have shown tremendous appreciation for that work, so much so that their interest inspired *More African American Special Days*. While some of the celebrations, for ease of access, have been given comparable titles in both *African American Special Days* and *More African American Special Days*, the content of each of the *More African American Special Days* services does not replicate those services found in *African American Special Days*. Thus, either "A Day for Renewing Men" (Volume II) or "Men's Day" (Volume I) may be used for celebrating Men's Day.

Like the original *Special Days*, this volume is dedicated to help enhance Black church programming and to reflect the elegant, faith-seeking, life-affirming, and freedom-longing people that we African Americans are. Each *Special Day* provides these elements: (a) Occasion; (b) Welcome; (c) Prayer; (d) Litany; (e) Vow of Commitment; (f) Suggested Colors; (g) Scriptures; and (h) Poem of Reflection.

Each service relies both on scripture and on the African American life experience, traditions, and history. The selected scriptures include a Hebrew Bible or Old Testament reading, a Psalm, Gospel, and an Epistle, with a focus on worship or service, love, trust or commitment, empowerment and transformation, as well as God's gifts to us. Where possible, I use African American persons to illustrate an attitude or commitment. These services bring together the powerful ritual and liturgical drama of the worship experience and our heritage that emerges from the African diaspora, and are tools to instill self and communal esteem and inspiration for religious, spiritual, health, and general education purposes. Most of the prayers and other statements provide spaces to insert the names of the church, related numbers or dates, or geographical places. These statements and prayers are to be tailored for your own church ceremony by including the names of honorees, the congregation, the community, or of helpful members where appropriate.

These services can be used as they appear in this volume or selected portions can be adapted within other program formats. For example, use the suggested colors in program design (for example, in the colors of bulletin board decorations, program, flowers, candles, or attire for the service). Incorporate the suggested scripture, in whole or in part, in the body of the program as a resource for theme development, or a tool for spiritual reflection and team building for the overall program committee. This volume is an invitation to you to create a stronger bond and sense of interconnectedness with the worship life and the daily life of your church.

I submit these ideas, prayers, litanies, and statements in a grateful, prayerful spirit of thanksgiving and love, to God's glory and for your use.

Lent 2004

OUR FAMILY AT
HOMECOMING AND REUNION

Occasion

Traditional African life is communal based. African Americans have retained the importance of community and family gatherings. Homecomings and family reunions have been long-standing celebrations, and that ritual practice received a huge boost with the publishing of Alex Haley's *Roots*, and the subsequent television movie series of the same name. Many African American families have extended families that go far beyond biological ties. Sometimes these extended families include neighbors, friends, and church family members. There are "play" aunts, uncles, nieces, and nephews; lots of Big Mamas, cousins, Grannies, Paw Paws, Lil Sises, Sisters, Ba' Brothers, and godparents. In thanksgiving and anticipation, we the members of *[name of the group, family, or church family]* rejoice in the gift of family, remember our ancestors, and are overjoyed at this *[family reunion or homecoming]*.

Today we honor the great heritage of family and community, the love that we share, the contributions we have made to the world, and the blessedness of life given us by God. By God's grace, we have been blessed with many generations; have celebrated weddings, births, anniversaries, graduations, and other rites of passage. We have stood by one another in difficult times, with deaths, losses, misfortune, and hardships. We cherish the gifts of families, church families, and the different communities that have supported us in life. We give thanks for all of these relationships and desire to be ever so faithful to each family and personal connection we have made along the way. We thank and bless God for the love, care, and support of family. Today we celebrate families; we give thanks for reunions, for times of renewal and strength. May we have many more.

Welcome

When the psalmist says, "Make a joyful noise unto the Lord," we know that it is time to offer praise and thanksgiving for all that God has done; it is time to worship. In joy and delight, we, the pastors, officers, and members of *[name of church]* and the *[name of homecoming or family reunion group]*, welcome you this day to worship, to be renewed, restored, and reconnected as we honor the *[homecoming or family reunion]* of *[name of church or name of family]*. As members of God's family, we come honoring God's loving, merciful relationship with us, and our relationship with each other. In gratitude, we welcome you today, to recall the many experiences you have had together, to honor those who have joined the ancestral chorus, and to bless all those who are present on this side of Jordan. Our home is your home; make yourselves comfortable and please let us know if there is anything we can do to make your visit more joyous.

On behalf of the [church, organization, or family name], we are so honored and blessed by your presence, and pray that you experience the peace and love of Christ Jesus as you worship with us today, and as you go forth in the world. As we gather today, we recall the gatherings of community circles in Africa, the secret gatherings for worship during slavery, and earlier reunions and times when our families have gathered in the past. We invite you to experience this service fully, to take our joy and love with you, and to hold on to your faith, the faith that can sustain you in the days ahead. Know that you are always welcome here in this holy place; you are one of us; be welcomed.

Prayer

O Divine, Holy God, you who called the world into being, you, who are the Architect of the Universe, the loving designer of all there is: we gather today in exquisite delight and adoration of you, giving all honor and praise to you, as we celebrate this [homecoming or reunion] worship service.

We come today in your honor, giving witness to all that you have done in our lives. You have given us many communities and many families who join today as one worshiping body. We give thanks that you love us so well and that you are so committed to being in relationship with us, that your compassion offers us a model that we can use to understand our relationships with others. We thank you for being in covenant with us; we pray to be able to be in covenant with others in our family.

We give thanks that daily, moment-by-moment, you look beyond our faults, and you never let our faults stop you from tending to our needs. We need your wisdom and strength to keep our families healthy; to help us get through the difficult times, the times that boggle our imagination, that just fail to make sense to us. Just as Jesus taught the disciples to pray, we pray for your rule over the world, we pray for the willingness to name the hurts done to us and for the gift of being able to forgive others so that we ourselves might be forgiven.

Help us have the faith of the mustard seed, that when all else fails, when our best efforts and hard work have not made a difference, our faith in you will sustain us through our journey. Help us place all of our cares and concerns on your altar, trusting in your love and mercy and your gift of healing. Help us avoid the practice of condemnation, understanding that you made us different, like flowers in a garden, like shells on the beach, like stars in the heavens. Help us respect life, the gift of our own lives, and the possibilities for transformation as we learn to walk, talk, plan, and pray together.

Litany

LEADER: Blessed, holy quietness, we stand in assurance of God's love for us and the blessing of family and community. In gratitude, we give thanks for life and each other.

PEOPLE: **We rejoice and give thanks for our ancestors, for our children, and for all family members and friends. We appreciate rituals and festivals that celebrate our lives together.**

LEADER: We celebrate the families of faithful church communities and celebrate those who have been guides for our communities: Paul Robeson, Daniel Coker, Vashti Murphy McKenzie, James Earl Massey, Manuel Scott, Sr., Cheryl Townsend Gilkes, Samuel Dewitt Proctor, Leontine Kelly, and J. Alfred Smith, Sr.

PEOPLE: **Many noble persons of God have given their lives and leadership to the up-building of God's kingdom and for justice: Charles H. Mason, Charles P. Jones, William Henry Miles, Ella Mitchell, Joseph A. Johnson, Jr., William Seymour, Peter Gomes, Marian Anderson, William Augustus Jones, Jr., and Shirley Ceasar.**

LEADER: As congregations and families, we celebrate the love for each other, the physical, mental, emotional, and spiritual traits that we share; the gift of friendship and relationship that makes joy and peace possible.

PEOPLE: **To God, we give all praise and glory for the marvelous blessings and challenges of family and community. We pray that we may better appreciate each day as if it were our last, each moment as if we would live for a lifetime.**

ALL: **For the grace of life, for the beauty of family and congregations, for the opportunity to celebrate our relationship with God and ourselves in community, we give thanks.**

Vow of Commitment

As we stand before the God of Simeon and Elijah, of Anna and Esther, we give you our deepest thanks and adoration, for you are worthy of praise. With your gift of life, we pledge to love our family members and ourselves. We honor our communities and will do all that we can to strengthen and protect them. We cry out with the voices of our ancestors that say, "Oh, Jesus Fix Me." When we are open to you fixing us, we become transformed and made anew. We are then able to put away destructive practices and embrace life-affirming behaviors that will honor our bodies, minds, and spirits so generously given to us by you. This day we celebrate ourselves and our communities, for the community has helped to train and mold us.

For communities and families everywhere we give thanks. We pray for the wisdom and divine guidance to help families and communities operate from a place of self-respect and respect for others. We trust that being grounded in your love, we can work together for the good of the whole; that we can learn to listen better, to be more tolerant and patient; to be kind, and to offer hospitality generously. Help us to create such a spiritual environment that many will receive rebirth and renewal, and that we will have a greater appreciation for the gifts of life, health, family, community, and love.

Suggested Colors

Green and red are the colors for homecoming and family reunions. Green symbolizes life, freshness, love, growth, healing, perspective, peace, visibility, and the divine. Red symbolizes living blood, love, emotion, strife, ardor, warmth, passion, and anger.

Scriptures

I will sing of your steadfast love, O LORD, forever; with my mouth I will proclaim your faithfulness to all generations. (Ps. 89:1)

God said, "This is the sign of the covenant that I make between me and you and every living creature that is with you, for all future generations: I have set my [rain]bow in the clouds, and it shall be a sign of the covenant between me and the earth." (Gen. 9: 12-13)

But Jesus refused, and said to him, "Go home to your friends, and tell them how much the Lord has done for you, and what mercy he has shown you." (Mark 5:19)

Now to [God] who by the power at work within us is able to accomplish abundantly far more than all we can ask or imagine, to [God] be glory in the church and in Christ Jesus to all generations, forever and ever. Amen. (Eph. 3:20-21)

Poem of Reflection

FAMILY RELATIONS: REUNION CELEBRATIONS

*Grands, great grands, and children, too
All come around at reunion time
Auntie, Uncle, and cousins twice removed
All come together so we can get in the groove
Of celebrations and remembering
Of laughter and tears
Of sweet potato pie, and a sock-it-to me cake
Iced tea, coffee, and warm handshakes.*

*Families are kin
Whose love we hold dear
We connect in major ways
At play, and church, around kitchen tables
We share stories and tall tales
We reminisce about what once was
Dream of what may come to be;
Families come in all shapes and sizes
Families are miracles in progress
Covenants with God and community.*

*Families enjoy reunions
We get to see who we're like
Our walk and talk
The shapes of our hands
Our laughter, our accent
Our big hearts and warm smiles;
Enjoy this reunion
Whether your first, perhaps your last.
Families are vital,
Celebrations invigorating
How blessed this
Marvelous tradition.*

A DAY TO HONOR
OUR MOTHERS

Occasion

Mothers come in many sizes, shapes, personalities, temperaments, and ages. Mothers are parents who may be biological, adoptive, and/or nurturing. Today, we join communities across the world in celebrating the gift of motherhood. In the Bible, God's activity is often that of a mother, reflecting strength, deep caring, nurturing, and tenderness. God holds us like a mother, bringing comfort, love, and a desire to be in healthy, intimate relationship. In honoring mothers today, we honor the mothers of *[name of church]*: *[list the names of mothers of the church]*.

Hannah, the mother of Samuel, prayed speaking with her heart, as she poured out her soul before the Lord, for the gift of a son, vowing to give him to the Lord for all the days of his life (1 Sam. 1:9-15). Caring mothers daily pray for their children, for the safety and comfort of all children everywhere. Many have borne the tremendous responsibility of being a mother for their families, communities, for the nation. Many women have been mothers to movements and to faith, educational, and literary communities, and we honor their contributions. Notably, Ella Pearson Mitchell advocates for the rights of black women to exercise their preaching gifts; Dorothy Height, founder of the Black Family Celebration, is a prime mover in the National Council of Negro Women. Johnnetta Cole has served as president of black women's colleges, Spelman and Bennett; Toni Morrison, as black female literary artist, has used African American women as symbols in her novels, which help us to examine the effects of racism, classism, sexism, and all those factors which blight a dream of a free and equal society.

Mothers of movements, communities, and families teach us much and share with us their mother wit, or wisdom to deal with everyday decisions. We are so grateful for the patience, love, and understanding that mothers give us; for the creativity they encourage in us; for the times they have stood by us, when all others have given up on us. We rejoice at the women in our lives who we know as godmother, grandmother, mother, sisters, spouse, Mo'Dear, Ma Ma, Mim, and Mee-Ma. We embrace the challenge this day of knowing that mothers are persons with their own needs, and that we are called not to take them for granted. May mothers love themselves enough to know how to say "No," and may we learn to appreciate them as gifts.

Welcome

Beloved sisters and brothers in Christ, we welcome you to this glorious celebration of mothers. We, the members

and family of *[name of church]* greet you with joy and an attitude of praise and thanksgiving. God has blessed us to see
another year; many of us have gone through valleys; some
of us have been on mountaintops. Some of us have become
mothers this year; others have mothers who have gone on
to be a part of the celestial chorus. Each of us can name
mothers who have been important in our lives. We carry
them in our hearts and their guidance and memories are
ever present with us.

Today we welcome you with delight and invite you to
think of them as we honor mothers today. On behalf of our
pastor, officers, and members of *[name of church]*, we open
our hearts and our church home to you. We extend to you
our hospitality and blessings of appreciation for being with
us today, for there are many other places you could be
today. We salute you who wear white flowers in memory of
mothers who have died. We salute you who wear red flowers in honor of those mothers who are living and serving on
this side of Jordan. We invite you to take this welcome and
share with others, honoring the precious gift of motherhood.

We extend a welcome to all mothers today, and all of
those who will give birth to new ideas, to new movements,
to nurturing communities, and the love and care of children.
We pray that the spirit you feel here, and the experiences
you have here will leave a deep impression of kindness and
compassion. You are welcome!

Prayer

Generous God of all Creation, from the time of ancient
Israel, through the middle passage, slavery, reconstruction,
the modern Civil Rights movement and on into the twenty-first century, you have been a mother to the motherless, a
companion, constant guide, and friend. Within scripture, we
see numerous examples of mothers who have nurtured others and brought messages of hope and promise. Tabitha was

a disciple who worked on behalf of the poor and was a disciple of many good works. Lois was a faithful grandmother and Eunice a faithful mother to Timothy. Milcah showed deep affection and support; Hannah was a woman of great piety. We are grateful for these mothers of faith and presence, whose witness provides guideposts for gracious behavior.

God of all mothers, we bless you for having given us the special role of mother in the lives of all persons. Help us to honor and support mothers and remember the importance of mothers having room to be themselves, above and beyond the role and duty of being a mother. Help mothers to not feel burdened by their responsibilities and bless them to have wisdom in parenting and mentoring. Bless them with a sense of humor and a great deal of lightheartedness, so that their frustrations will not result in anger, abuse, or destructive behavior toward themselves and others. Bless our church family with the insight to help support mothers by precept and example toward a life of balance.

Litany

LEADER: This day we honor the gift and office of motherhood, in its many forms toward the up-building of the rule of God throughout the world.

PEOPLE: **May we grasp a vision of motherhood that helps our community flourish, do justice, and love mightily, that we can honor the glory of God in all mothers.**

LEADER: We bless and praise you protecting God, who knows us and our mothers in intimate ways, calling us to relationships with mothers of honesty and affirmation.

PEOPLE: **As we affirm mothers of the world today, we pray for their strength, their comfort, and the peace and wellness of their souls, minds, and bodies.**

LEADER: In deep appreciation, we affirm our mothers, with respect, joy, and hope. May mothers, their children and families, of all kinds, be in dialogue, listen well to each other, and be the holy presence of Christ for each other in their midst.

PEOPLE: We honor the voices, ideas, dreams, desires, and contributions of all mothers. We pray continuously for their health and strength, that they find motherhood, in its many manifestations, a source of fulfillment, acknowledgment, and bliss.

ALL: We pray for those who desire to be mothers and have not yet experienced their fulfillment; we pray for those who have known deep pain as mothers, that they will experience redemption and peace. May all mothers have a mother who can be fully present for them. In the name of Christ Jesus, we bless and give thanks to mothers.

Vow of Commitment

God of our mothers, ancient and modern, we praise you and bless you, that you care for us and love us so deeply to honor us with the gift of mothers. In our roles as mothers, may we have the dignity and presence of singer Lena Horne; may we have the grace and agility in body and spirit of a Wilma Rudolph; may we respect our proud oral African tradition like Ruby Dee. We accept the challenges of being mothers and being mothered; we are grateful for them as our role models, for they sustain and support us.

As mothers, we invite the anointing of the Holy Spirit, to empower us with the strength and grace to live a spiritual life, where we put God first in everything we do. We give praise and honor to God for the opportunity to serve in the ministry of motherhood, made in God's image, where we live as guardians, teachers, and leaders. We offer our-selves on behalf of our families and communities as those chosen by God to live a life of loving-kindness and mercy. We cherish moments with our children as special times of unspeakable joy, where we share a legacy of wisdom for all the ages.

We appreciate that some are called to be mothers and serve tirelessly. Some have desired to be mothers and have had the grace of walking with friends, family, and commu-nity in other ways. Some have given birth, but failed to live out the call of motherhood. We recommit this day to honor the role of mother and to appreciate mothers in every walk of life. We pray that all biological, extended, adopted, play, and godmothers have the peace that passes all understand-ing as they love themselves, love others, set priorities, honor boundaries, and experience grace in the little things of life.

Suggested Colors

Yellow and orange are the colors for Mother's Day. Yellow suggests liveliness, animation, radiance, good cheer, wisdom, knowledge, intelligence, inspiration, and a reflec-tion of God's glory. Orange symbolizes the earth, autumn, warmth, fruitfulness, cheerfulness, and richness.

Scriptures

But you, O LORD, are a God merciful and gracious, slow to anger and abounding in steadfast love and faithfulness. (Ps. 86:15)

You shall love the Lord your God with all your heart, and with all your soul, and with all your [strength]. (Deut. 6:5)

You will know them by their fruits. Are grapes gathered from thorns, or figs from thistles? (Matt. 7:16)

Now, however, that you have come to know God, or rather to be known by God, how can you turn back again to the weak and beggarly elemental spirits? How can you want to be enslaved to them again? (Gal. 4:9)

Poem of Reflection

MOTHERS: JEWELS OF THE NILE

Exquisite, powerful giants
Sprung from a land ancient and remarkable
The fount of civilization itself ~ Africa;
More delicate than the finest pearl
More resplendent than the Hope diamond,
More valuable than gold
Distinctive, made of royalty
Radiant flowers of the world.

The power of Mothers
Reflect the depths and power of the mighty Mississippi,
The mystery and awesomeness of Niagara Falls,
The ability to lean yet stand firm like the Tower of Pisa,
The dedication and love embodied in the Taj Mahal,
The freedom and tenacity symbolized in the Lincoln Memorial
The inviting nature and the nobility of the Statue of Liberty.

Mothers, the delight of our hearts
Make us feel good about ourselves
Support us in our hobbies and dreams,
Cuddle us when we need a hug
Discipline us when we need clarity;
Listen to our secrets
Provide guidance when needed
Share laughter when we need to smile
Always welcome us with understanding.

As we need mothers,
Mothers need us;
We salute you, and adore you;
We thank God for you;
Mother, you're the best.

A DAY TO HONOR
OUR FATHERS

Occasion

Majestic God of life and all blessings, today we come to celebrate the gift of fathers. Fathers are near and dear to our hearts. We have all kinds of fathers, young, old, and middle-aged; some have jolly laughs and a keen sense of humor; some are serious and shy; some are athletic; some are distinguished gentlemen; some are terrific chefs who make our favorite dishes. Some fathers read us stories as children; some gave us a ride on the first day of school; some are terrific mechanics and plumbers; some fathers just make us feel good about ourselves.

We learn about fathers in magazines, novels, and in scripture. The Bible tells the stories of different types of fathers, some who seemed to love well, and some who seemed to be misguided. Jacob truly loved Joseph, but did he ignore his other sons? Jephthah was a man of faith, but carelessly caused the death of his daughter. Joshua committed himself and his family to serving the Lord. Job taught his children, by example, that the most important acts in life were to worship God and to be honest and pious. Cornelius nurtured his family's well-being, liberally gave to the poor, and prayed constantly.

Many African American men have served as fathers of movements. Charles H. Houston and Thurgood Marshall were fathers of jurisprudence and the quest for justice; James Forten had great influence as an abolitionist and entrepreneur. Martin R. Delaney was a father of Black Nationalism. Henry Highland Garnet, Gabriel Prosser, Denmark Vesey, Robert Young, and David Walker were abolitionists and fathers of black liberation theology. [Names of local fathers] are fathers in our community.

Today we honor and celebrate fathers and are grateful for their love, tenacity, wisdom, care—for being who they are. We celebrate fathers as mighty men of God, who relate to us as godfathers, grandfathers, fathers, brothers, and spouses; as Dad, pawpaw, Poppa, and Pops. We pray for the transformation of all so-called deadbeat dads. We pray God's blessings on all fathers, that they might be all that God has called them to be, that together we can be a loving family.

Welcome

We come in adoration and thanksgiving, to honor the One who woke us up this morning and started us on our way. In joy and gratitude, we the pastor, officers, and members of [name of church] welcome you with open hearts to this Father's Day celebration. Along with other communities throughout the United States, we invite you to join us in affirming and acknowledging the gifts, responsibilities, and privileges of being a father. We recognize godfathers, grandfathers, fathers, sons, brothers, and male friends who serve in the role of father: one who offers guidance, love, support, nurture, and a shoulder to lean on. We salute you who wear white flowers in memory of fathers who have died. We salute you who wear red flowers in honor of those fathers who are living and serving on this side of Jordan. We invite you to take this welcome and share with others, honoring the precious gift of fatherhood.

We welcome you to think of all adoptive, biological, and extended fathers who have influenced your life; your presence with us today honors them. We hold in prayer the memory of those fathers whose strength helped our ancestors survive middle passage, slavery, reconstruction, Jim Crow, and the ongoing reality of oppression because of the God-given hues of our skin. We give thanks for the fathers who, like Joshua, have vowed to serve the Lord. May the preaching, teaching, singing, and praying inspire and uplift you. May our honoring fathers today help you recall warm memories; may old wounds begin to heal. On this sacred day, as we honor fathers, we welcome you to this house consecrated for God's service; we welcome you to our spiritual home. We are here to serve and bless you. You are welcome!

Prayer

Gentle and charitable God, you have created the ministry of father as a source of strength, kindness, leadership, and compassion. We stand in this holy moment making a joyful noise, lifting songs and praise to you for the gift of fathers for their support and direction. We praise you for being a father to the fatherless and for inspiring men to be surrogate dads and big brothers to those who stand in need. You are there for us in ways our human fathers could not be.

You have given us life, health, and strength, creativity, community, and family, along with the desire to be the best fathers possible.

We ask special blessings for all fathers today. We pray that no weapons formed against them can prosper (Isa. 54:17); particularly those fathers who are serving in the military forces and with law enforcement, who are often in harm's way, protecting us, our families, and our country, those fathers who are incarcerated, and for those fathers who are imprisoned to any person, place, or thing that causes destruction of self-esteem and of family relationships. We pray for wisdom and special insight for fathers that they may be clear about who they are, and whose they are; that they can appreciate their children for who they are without trying to relive their lives through them. We share the hopes that fathers can engage in dialogue with wives, partners, children, and families; knowing when to listen, and when to speak; when to pray and when to act—in all things, at all times, being prayerful, devoted men of God.

Litany

LEADER: On this day that God has ordered, we celebrate the ministry of all fathers, everywhere, to the awe-inspiring glory of God.

PEOPLE: **For the gifts and responsibilities of fatherhood, we humble ourselves to be better equipped to honor this ministry and to pray God's blessings on fathers everywhere.**

LEADER: For special, warm memories of fathers, for their sharing, for their going the extra mile to support their family, church, and community, we give thanks.

PEOPLE: **We lift up our voices in deep regard for fathers who have dreamed dreams and had great visions that have helped our people experience more justice and equality.**

LEADER: In love of God and of life, in honor of the role of protector, visionary, and friend, we salute fathers, asking God to make their way plain, and lessen all pain.

PEOPLE: **Help fathers to blossom in self-esteem and in satisfaction over little things; help them experience forgiveness for all wrongdoing and experience your hope toward the possibility for change.**

ALL: **O Emmanuel, we come to rejoice for all fathers and all who interact with fathers, as a gift of life, of vitality. We pray for all parents, communities, and agencies of social outreach that they might better affirm the role and gift of father.**

Vow of Commitment

O God Everlasting, the God who sees and loves, we stand before you today in joy and meekness, for you are awesome and so powerful. We stand in solidarity with fathers, and especially honor the fathers of [name of church]. We know that you hold us responsible for our well-being and that of our communities; we pledge our trust to stand strong in the Lord, one day at a time as we embrace all of the responsibilities of fatherhood. In thanksgiving for the faithfulness of God, we promise to be faithful to our task of parenting, of being partners and lovers, of being men of faith.

Lord, help us to be the fathers you have called us to be; to be the men of integrity, placing our allegiance to you before all things; being guided by our commitment to you, the commitment formalized in our baptism. We pledge to live life as a holy walk, for you have made us in your image, thus you shape us with sacred hands to participate in life as a sacred journey. We pledge to eat and drink, work and play in moderation. We will be thoughtful parents and leaders; we will stand up for Jesus and for our families. We take responsibility for being good stewards of our gifts, graces, time, and tithes so that we are prepared to help share the gospel wherever we go.

Suggested Colors

Blues and red are the colors for Father's Day. Blue suggests peace, serenity, calm, work, space, royalty, and tends to be a unifying, healing element. Red symbolizes grandeur, life, courage, love, passion, and living blood.

Scriptures

In you our ancestors trusted; they trusted and you delivered them. (Ps. 22:4)

I was a father to the needy, and I championed the cause of the stranger. (Job 29:16)

Take my yoke upon you, and learn from me; for I am gentle and humble in heart, and you will find rest for your souls. (Matt. 11:29)

By contrast, the fruit of the Spirit is love, joy, peace, patience, kindness, generosity, faithfulness, gentleness, and self-control. There is no law against such things. (Gal. 5:22-23)

Poem of Reflection

FATHERS: WORKS IN PROCESS

Do you call him Dad or Pops or Father?
Is he so tall in your eyes that he's larger than a mountain?
His voice so deep that it lies on the ocean floor?
His walk so gentle, that he's by your side before you know it?
Is he your hero or your enemy?
Your mentor or your parole officer?
Is he all these things all rolled into one?

Dads, fathers are like us ~
Strong and weak, smart yet naive sometimes,
Sometimes blind when it comes to their weaknesses
Sometimes minimizing the depths of their strengths;
Dads are in the process of becoming;
And we can help them in their walk.

Dads need words of encouragement
Need to know that they matter to us
For more than a paycheck;
For more than being a breadwinner or sperm donor
Dads have deep feelings, they love deeply
Whether they speak these words or not.
Watch a dad with his child
And never have you seen such a beaming smile
Coming from deep within;
Watch a dad with his mother
There's a gentle touch and deep admiration for Mama;
That's our dads; our fathers
Men of distinction,
Called by God,
As stewards from Christ
They are noble creatures
Needing to love others,
Needing to be loved.

So everyday is father's day
When we love our dad's well.
When we respect our fathers enough
To let them know we care.

A DAY FOR
RENEWING WOMEN

Occasion

On this marvelous [*spring, summer, autumn, winter*] day,
we come to celebrate the [*number*] annual Women's Day program of [*name of church*]. This is a time of sharing and honoring the energy, gifts, and contributions of girls and women
in the life of our faith community. Their contributions are
tremendous, and it is important that we not take their ministries for granted. The women of [*name of church*] participate in all areas of ministry and emulate the strengths and
wisdom of many biblical women, like Queen Vashti, Sister
Miriam, Prophet Anna, and Deaconess Phoebe.

We stand with and in honor of the women of [*name of
church*], as they listen with great discernment, waiting on

the Lord to renew their strength; that they might mount up with wings like eagles, run and not get weary, walk and not faint (Isa. 40:31). With the wisdom from our mothers in Africa, from those through slavery and the modern Civil Rights era, women continue to go forth in prophecy, in love, in dedication for the work of Christ Jesus. With the forethought of Anna Julia Cooper, the jubilance for God of Mahalia Jackson, the tenacity and commitment of Prathia Hall, and the poetic splendor of Pauli Murray, we lead and are led, sing and study well, preach and listen fervently for the leadings of God as we minister in grace and peace to God's people. Blessed be!

Welcome

To the pastor, all distinguished pulpit guests, officers, members of [name of church] and visiting friends, we greet you in the glorious name of Christ Jesus! Some of you have come from many miles, some of you are visiting for the first time, some of you were born here or married in this church, others have come by invitation of friends and family. All of us have gathered here today, by God's grace and we have come to worship, in word and song. We come making ourselves a holy offering to God in thanksgiving for the blessings of life, health, and strength. We come praising and rejoicing as we honor our women and their powerful ministries of love and compassion. We welcome you today and invite you to experience the living gospel of Christ in a new way, as a message of affirmation and inspiration, of hope and anticipation.

We the women of [name of church] are honored that, of all of the churches you could have visited today, you chose to come and visit us. We herald a rich legacy of a diversity of gifts, from the appreciation of life and protest of Ida B. Wells-Barnett, to the entrepreneurial savvy of Madame C. J. Walker, from the stance for women's rights of a Mary

Church Terrell, to the love for the folk of Zora Neale Hurston. We are overjoyed with your presence here and acknowledge that your presence blesses us tremendously. In honoring all women, we also honor their lives, their creativity, their wisdom, and their ability to stand as daughters, sisters, mothers, grandmothers, and friends. Our church home is your church home. You are welcome here. Please avail yourselves of our worship, our concern, ourselves. Welcome, welcome, welcome.

Prayer

Beloved God of the Universe, with joyous hope and spiritual anticipation, we come to this service with prayerful hearts, thanking you for your majesty, your compassion, your love, and generous mercy. Have mercy upon us as we come with expressions of love, care, and concern. Some of us have heavy hearts, are experiencing grief and deep loss. We mourn for loved ones and we mourn for all of the children who are unloved, abused, and misunderstood. We yearn to do your will in our daily lives and desire to help lead others to the power of your love. We thank you for being a rock in a weary land, a shelter in the time of storm, a way-maker, and a heart-regulator.

Help us to walk in your beautiful light, strong of mind, body, and soul. May this Women's Day celebration emulate all that is holy and kind. Help us to form stronger connections as we work with one another. Help us face our differences with an openness for growth and change. Help us grow stronger in faith, and be inclusive in our programming of women in our larger community. Help us, like Ruth, be loyal and compassionate without being a footstool; help us, like Elizabeth, experience the awesomeness of the Holy Spirit with loud cries of joy. Make this moment holy, and the fruits of this time together long lasting. For these and all other blessings we give thanks. Amen.

Litany

LEADER: With gracious hope, we praise your name, standing in one accord as women of faith, to work together as recruits for Christ to spread peace at home and in the world.

PEOPLE: As women of faith, we stand like trees planted by the water, for we will not be moved from our mission to love the Lord, and to love ourselves and each other.

LEADER: With respect and awe, we await your call on our lives to serve this present age, our calling to fulfill as joyful women, in our strength and in our frailty.

PEOPLE: As women of joy, like Mother Hale, who took care of crack addicted babies in Harlem, we say yes to our calling to be missionaries of Christ, to minister to the sick and shut in, to those weary of life, to those needing words of encouragement, to know they are loved.

LEADER: Like Lorraine Hansberry, we cry out for the total liberation of all God's people, of African peoples all over the world, that we all might work for justice and experience freedom and equality.

PEOPLE: With the voices of poets and prophets, of friends and family, we women of faith believe in your power to change hardened hearts, in your love for us, and the possibility for violence and evil doings to be overcome in the world.

ALL: As your eyes, ears, and bodies in the world, we give honor to you as we embrace your ministry to work

together for change. Help us love others when we do not like them, embrace forgiveness without forgetting indignities, experience intimacy with you in a way that shapes all of our relationships toward the health and good of all.

Vow of Commitment

As women of faith, and of God, we recommit ourselves this day to a ministry of transformation that moves us to be arbiters for justice and freedom. As members of the body of Christ, we rejoice and give thanks that God cares for us still and has made a way for us to participate in the building up of community. We take seriously that message Christ first gave to Mary Magdalene at his Resurrection, to "go into all the world and proclaim the good news to the whole creation" (Mark 16:15). In that light, we promise to:

- pray first and listen in anticipation for God's leading in our personal endeavors and in our ministry for the church;
- be active participants in all aspects of the work you have called us to, in the church itself and in the larger society;
- help others, when they are like us or when they are different, that they might be open to experience their full potential as beings lovingly created;
- face the challenges of life and of ministry, being open to the support of family and friends, able to go through, without giving up;
- affirm others and graciously accept kind words and helpful suggestions from those trusted friends who seek to support our divine call.

Looking to the present, not worrying about the past or being anxious about the future, we stand balanced in the love of Christ, releasing all greed, envy, shame, and guilt. We boldly embrace our gifts, study well to grow in wisdom, take time to play and have a balanced life.

As women of hope and new life, we embrace our gift of salvation and redemption; we pledge to express ourselves magnificently, in the brilliant, loving, powerful, creative, beautiful manner that God has made us, to proclaim peace and possibility.

Suggested Colors

Pink and black are the colors for Women's Day. Pink (rose, fuchsia, or hot pink) denotes warmth, welcome, passion, high spirits. Black symbolizes solidarity, strength, power, infinity.

Scriptures

Praise the LORD! I will give thanks to the LORD with my whole heart, in the company of the upright, in the congregation. (Ps. 111:1)

Thus says the LORD of hosts: Render true judgments, show kindness and mercy to one another. (Zech. 7:9)

Her neighbors and relatives heard that the Lord had shown . . . great mercy to her, and they rejoiced with her. (Luke 1:58)

Therefore, since we are justified by faith, we have peace with God through our Lord Jesus Christ. (Rom. 5:1)

Poem of Reflection

WOMEN: ANOINTED, SACRED, AWESOME

Women—glorious, magnificent, anointed
The power of the Holy Spirit
Cascading over her crown,
Her unseen halo, capping
Mystery, desire, willingness
To be strong, yet weak
Powerful, yet a team player
Beautiful inwardly
Gentle of spirit when needed
Angry and forceful when
Protecting her world.

Woman, sacred, of God
In God's image
Not less than a man
Nor an appendage,
For full and complete is she
In and of herself
For God made her that way;
Elegant, beautiful, strong, faithful;
A vast flower garden, diverse of color
Many personalities, many gifts, many graces.
Oft complicated, oft straightforward
Hasten not to assume
You know who she is.

Woman, awesome
Wonderful, commanding, imaginative
Sensual, elegant,
Of earth and heaven combined.
Made in God's image
A gathering, listening community
Of those faithful, and willing
To go where needed,
To lead and follow
To be gifted, elegant, and free.

A DAY FOR
RENEWING MEN

Occasion

To the pastor, officers, members, and visiting friends of *[name of church]:* what a glorious day this is to celebrate this Day of Renewal for Men. What a joyous event in the life of our church and community. We have come to honor and lift up the boys and men of our church family, in the name of Jesus through the anointing of the Holy Spirit. Experiencing our lives as gifts, we come with gratitude and thanksgiving to honor the sons, brothers, husbands, fathers, and other men who mentor, befriend, and support us in our lives and ministries. We salute all members of the body of Christ, and witness to the contributions of boys and men in their journeys of faith.

How glorious that we come to worship God and to celebrate Men's Day. With the faith of Abraham, the humility of Moses, the hospitality of Jethro, the wisdom of Simeon, and the priestly walk of Melchizedek we come to worship and build community. We offer prayers for peace and fellowship in the world. We offer songs as balm in Gilead to soothe the wounded spirits of human hearts. We now acknowledge the boys and men of *[name of church]*, of *[city, state]*, of the world as we experience renewal, hope, love, joy, and recommitment to God's call on our lives.

As *[name of one of your church's founders]* had a dream about this church, as Nelson Mandela persevered, as Richard Allen stood for dignity, as Joseph A. Johnson, Jr. was a preacher/scholar, as Maynard Jackson led Atlanta as mayor, we celebrate dreams, visions, leadership, and new possibilities in all that we do this day.

Welcome

To the pastor, officers, members, and friends of *[name of church]*: this is the day that the Lord has made, and in joyous celebration, we come to honor and glorify God, and we welcome each and every one of you for this momentous occasion. God has blessed us and the men of this church and called them to greatness, service, and leadership. We welcome you as a child of God, as one made in the image of God, who has come to join us in honoring and glorifying God. Our joy is tremendous and great is our anticipation of what will unfold during this worship service. We have come to celebrate another day of living, another opportunity to hear the Word of God, and a time to recognize the contribution of men and boys to *[name of church]*.

Let Mount Zion rejoice as we come to this holy place to praise! We have come to give thanks for the Lord's righteousness, to sing praise to God's name, the Most High (Ps. 7:17, author's paraphrase). This Most High God got us up this morning and started us on our way. We are so amazed that the God who sits high, also looks low, and cares about us. How can we do anything but praise?

We, the men of [name of church] welcome you, once, twice, three times! We thank you for coming today that we might share these honors with you, as we also honor other men of African descent who have made tremendous contributions to our world: Benjamin Mays, president of Morehouse; Howard Thurman, mystic and international peacemaker. We honor Jackie Robinson, athlete par excellence; educator and founder of Black History celebrations Carter G. Woodson; and bibliophile and collector of African American artifacts and print materials, the Sherlock Holmes of Negro History, Arthur Schomburg. We welcome you and invite you to experience new hope and new dreams with the men of this church. Your home is our home; please avail yourselves of our hospitality. May something that you see and experience here warm your heart and spirit. Welcome.

Prayer

Loving God of future hope and God of past triumphs over difficult times, we come to worship you, honor you, and adore you. Like Israel, we assemble in this sanctuary as a testimony to your faithfulness and tremendous grace. You have anointed men of old and men today to help spread the gospel, to witness to your awesome goodness and loving-kindness. You are God from everlasting to everlasting and continue to hold us in your care. Your mercy and graciousness is overwhelming and powerful. We thank you for who you are and all that you do, and for giving us the insight and guidance to celebrate this [number] annual Men's Day celebration at [name of church].

Noble God, we ask for your blessings on this program. May all the words and deeds we engage reflect your character, and bring healing within the gathered body of Christ. As we lift up the men of this congregation and this community, help us remember the thousands of men incarcerated in prisons, and for those outside of prison who are in the jails of addiction, violence, and emotional and mental pain and anguish. Show us how to walk with boys and men in our communities, to help them face their feelings and their pain, before they react with acts of violence on themselves or others.

Merciful One, help us as a community stand in the gap for those who are fatherless, for those who have no sons yet desire them, for those who have no husbands yet want them, for those who have no male friends but want one. Help us live an infectious life of joy, faith, and hope where we do not force our male children to be men before their time. Help us create positive, nurturing church communities where men will feel affirmed and empowered. Help us walk in wisdom in all relationships, in all church matters, and community outreach. Bless us to be men of conviction and distinction. All honor, glory, and praise be unto you. Amen.

Litany

LEADER: God of power and might, of love and justice, we celebrate and affirm men of God, as they work on behalf of ordained and lay ministries to love your people well.

PEOPLE: **By your grace, with renewed commitment and confidence, O God of Jacob, we offer ourselves as workers in your vineyards of hope and salvation. We come before your presence in anticipation, that we might love our neighbor and ourselves, as a community of faithful to fulfill the ministry of men in your honor.**

LEADER: In faith, like Franklin Frazier, we seek wisdom, we tell the truth about social realities, own up to the indictment that we have a growing black underclass; like Samuel Cornish, we work to help distribute the good news of the African American community.

PEOPLE: **Like Frazier, we call for awareness and change; like Cornish we call for more truth-telling and positive reinforcement for all those in our communities.**

LEADER: In service, like Tom Skinner, we understand that Christian ministry extends beyond formal church worship and evangelism needs to be expanded to those in college and in corporations, including organized sports; like Thomas Dorsey, we know that even as men, we can admit our pain and prayerfully share with God and trusted friends.

PEOPLE: **Together, we commit to doing outreach and community empowerment that can make a difference in the lives of the community of faith, lifting as we climb.**

ALL: **In thanksgiving, we rejoice, honoring men, ancient and modern; men made in the image of God, called to love and serve, to share and live the gospel in faith. Blessed be God forever.**

Vow of Commitment

Today, on this great occasion, we recommit ourselves to a life of faith, to the adoration, service, and love of God, and to the renewal and growth of the church and our spiritual journeys together. We accept our calling to fulfill Christ's message to us, to love God and our neighbor, to share the gospel, and to participate in love with our church family. We pledge in earnest:

To live and embrace a compassion for building community and for helping mentor our youth in ways to help them sustain their faith;

To share our testimonies of life and faith, in ways that can help inspire others to place God at the center of their lives;

To be good stewards of our time and our financial resources, as part of our daily spiritual growth and well-being;

To participate in the lay ministries of the church, with a willingness to learn and grow, taking courses and studying materials that can enhance our involvement in our church community;

To serve others, listen with patience, and set high standards as we both forgive and are willing to be forgiven, by the grace of God.

As followers of Christ Jesus, we put on the armor of God that we might stand against all powers and principalities (Eph. 6:11, 12). With the mantle of Christ, we recommit to a life of faith in love, where we do no harm to ourselves or to others. We renew the vows we took at our baptism to be one in faith with Christ and with the witnessing community of the church. We confess our faith and vow to follow God as our guide, our stronghold, our blessed Creator.

Suggested Colors

Green and blue are the suggested colors for this day of Renewal for Men. Green denotes steadiness, thoughtfulness, freshness, healing, peace, visibility, growth, and the divine. Blue denotes serenity, space, coolness, peacemaking, work, and unity.

Scriptures

Trust in the LORD and do good; so you will live in the land, and enjoy security. (Ps. 37:3)

[From Israel to God] *"In your steadfast love you led the people whom you redeemed; you guided them by your strength to your holy abode."* (Exod. 15:13)

But as for what was sown on good soil, this is the one who hears the word and understands it, who indeed bears fruit and yields, in one case a hundredfold, in another sixty, and in another thirty. (Matt. 13:23)

So we are ambassadors for Christ, since God is making [God's] appeal through us; we entreat you on behalf of Christ, be reconciled to God. (2 Cor. 5:20)

Poem of Reflection

MEN: NOBILITY WITH DISTINCTION

Men, young and old
Stand with distinction
As followers of Christ Jesus
Lived out in the church and the world;
To be lights of the world
Reflecting grace and mercy
Honoring life as gift
Strong of heart,
Gentle in spirit
Rooted in love.

Men of distinction
Walking tall for Christ
In bodies large and small
Even when seated
Radiate a presence of the divine
Releasing the fears of doubt and anguish;
Of blame, greed, and control
Toward a higher calling
Made sanctified by God.

Men of distinction
Of many different hues,
Complex ideas, histories, realities—
Let not your heart be troubled;
For God loves you unconditionally;
And as such, empowers you always
To be, to grow, to live, to give
To be, to receive, to thrive, magnificently.

YOUTH RITE OF PASSAGE DAY

Occasion

Rites of passage are significant moments in our lives, where we mark a time when we come to a threshold or turning point. These moments are often recognized through formal celebrations. These celebrations help the individuals and their communities take time out to observe their movement into a new and different phase of life. With this Rite of Passage comes a new place and new responsibilities in the society and in the church. In many Christian communities, the age of twelve is known as the age of reckoning, the age when a child passes into adulthood. Just as the Hebrew communities celebrate Bar and Bat Mitzvahs, many Christian communities confer their sacrament of Confirmation at this age. Jesus was twelve years old when he spoke with the rabbis and scholars in the temple.

Our celebration today honors the rite of passage from *[childhood to youth or youth to young adult]*. We thank God for life, transitions, and change. As our young people move from *[childhood or youth or young adults]* they will have to make adjustments as they separate from old habits and thoughts to learn new ways of being. They are in transition as they learn the new behaviors for this new phase of life that they are now entering. Then they will be able to experience incorporation, as they move completely into the new roles and ways of being. With love and nurture, our *[youth or young adults]* will stand stronger in their faith, embracing their responsibilities to follow the paths of Jesus Christ, empowered by the Holy Spirit.

Welcome

According to Ecclesiastes, we are seasonal people, for there is a time, a place, and a season for everything under the sun. We are so delighted that this is a season of celebrating the gifts and blessing of our youth. On behalf of the pastor, officers, and members of *[name of church]*, we are privileged to welcome you to praise the Lord, be restored, and experience our joy as we commemorate the rite of passage ceremony for our *[youth or young adults]*. We come to celebrate as a community of faith, to worship and recognize this time of transition in our congregation. We welcome you to join us in honoring the challenges, changes, and new beginnings in store for our *[youth or young adults]*, as they continue to grow into maturity.

This rite of passage marks the coming of age of our *[youth or young adults]* as they recall and remember the past and look forward to the future. Many of them have now faced the death of a loved one, have left or soon will be leaving home, and are beginning to make decisions on their own. We are here today to recognize this significant time in the life of our children and our community. This is a time to celebrate friendships, hopes, and dreams. We thank you so much for being a part of our worship service today. You are welcome to return at any time. As we celebrate this rite of passage, we pray that you will know the grace of God and the power of the Holy Spirit as you experience your own journeys and transitions in the days to come. You are welcome!

Prayer

Most noble and awesome God, we give thanks for you and for the gift of this day and this celebration where we honor life's transitions. We pray that you anoint our youth with love for family, for you, and themselves that they may be healthy and open to the love and counsel of others; that all children, adults, and seniors experience the love of Christ at home and within our church community as they experience various transitions in life. We ask that you grant us steadfast faith as a community so that we can be in unity, one with each other, putting our total trust and confidence in you. Help us to experience life and transitions, births, deaths, weddings, graduations, with grace and love. Please be present with us, hold us, and comfort us, that we might love others in turn. To you, O God, we give glory and praise.

O Loving One, as we work daily to be faithful to our covenant with you, we face many powers and principalities, that we cannot handle by ourselves as we experience various transitions, even those from morning to noon, and noon to midnight. We ask for the anointing of the Holy Spirit, that we might stand shaped by truth, held by righteousness, as we walk in peace, shielded by faith, draped by salvation, and steadfast in your scriptures (Eph. 6:10-19). As we move from childhood to our teen years, from teen years to that of young adult, from young adult to middle age, from middle age to our golden senior years, let us never forget whose we are—your children in covenant. Be with us this day, as our light, our path, our bread, our love, our heart, our body, our soul, our strength: one in unity, as we celebrate our differences, as we celebrate the gifts of time and change.

Litany

LEADER: Wonderful God, counselor and parent to us all, we rejoice and give thanks for the gifts of time and change that you have so honored in our lives.

PEOPLE: **We honor the lives of young people who have made significant contributions in our world, making it a better place. We acknowledge those young people who lost their lives and became martyrs for the 1960s Civil Rights movement.**

LEADER: We salute all children who volunteer and assist in hospitals, nursing homes, at camps for those with disabilities; those who help in after-school programs; who help with their younger relatives; who help in churches and society through Scouts, and other youth organizations.

PEOPLE: **We lift up the names of Addie Mae Collins, Cynthia Wesley, Carole Robertson, and Denise McNair, children murdered because cowardly terrorists set off a bomb at the Sixteenth Street Baptist Church, Birmingham, Alabama, where the girls attended Sunday school on September 18, 1963.** *

---

* The four suspects in the September 15, 1963 Sixteenth Street Baptist Church bombing were Robert E. Chambliss, Thomas Blanton, Jr., Bobby Frank Cherry, and Herman Cash. Herman Cash died in 1994 without ever being charged for his alleged participation in the bombing. In 1977 Robert E. Chambliss, a resident of Birmingham and longtime member of the Klan, was tried and convicted for his role in the bombing, and he died in prison in 1985. Thirty-nine years after the bombing Thomas Blanton, Jr. was convicted on four counts of first-degree murder—one count for each child. Bobby Frank Cherry was sentenced to life in prison in 2002. http://afroamhistory.about.com/library/weekly/aa051401.htm

LEADER: We honor the life and legacy of Emmett Till, a young teen from Chicago, Illinois, who was murdered while visiting his uncle the summer of 1955, in Money, Mississippi, for whistling (or saying "bye baby") to a white woman.

PEOPLE: **We acknowledge the children of the world today, those orphaned because of famine and AIDS, who are homeless, who need someone to pray for them, someone to love them. We give thanks for those children who are loved, who then extend themselves to help others.**

ALL: **Let us prayerfully recommit ourselves to the survival and nurture of all children. Let us appreciate the gift of children and never take them for granted. Let us embrace them, commit time to them, and create the rituals to help them graciously face the many transitions they will meet in their lives.**

Vow of Commitment

God of all youth and children everywhere, we are so grateful that you have made us in your image, that we praise you, bless you, and adore you. As young people, we desire to know you better and to come to love you more and more; may we be blessed with families who love and support us; may we stand proud in our heritage and be able to contribute to better the lives of many. We come to this time of transition and really need your love and comfort, O God, for this is a time where we are so vulnerable; we are both excited about the changes that are coming, and a little afraid. We pledge to honor you in all things and go to our parents, our pastors, and other responsible adults when we need help.

As young believers, we invite the anointing of the Holy Spirit to give us the strength and wisdom to live a spiritual life, at school, work, and play; at home, and at church. We thank God for the opportunity to serve in the ministry of Jesus Christ. We are grateful for this rite of passage, a time to celebrate and commemorate this time of transition in our lives. We care for youth who are not as fortunate as we are, for those who do not have anyone to pray for them. We vow to share the gospel by the way we live our lives, and to share the loving experiences of God with others. We offer ourselves to be role models and to let adults we trust know when one of our friends is hurting or in trouble.

We are so grateful for our lives and for a supportive, loving church family. In honor of that family and the time they have invested in us, we wish to invest time in those who come after us. We commit to Bible study, and to participate in various ministries in the church; these activities will enable us to take our full responsibility within the congregation. As we are in transition from childhood to that of teens, and later young adults, we promise to live each day to the fullest, as vessels of God. We invite your prayers that we may be steadfast, and grounded in our faith. Pray for us that we will not yield to temptation. We recommit ourselves during this day set aside to recognize the importance of a rite of passage, as we cross over to a time of new responsibilities, different expectations, times of new hopes and dreams, of more maturity and possibilities. We pray that all youth can have such support, and the blessing of experiencing a rite of passage to signal an ecclesiastic moment: a time of change in hope.

Suggested Colors

Orange and green are the suggested colors for celebrating the rite of passage for youth or young adults. Orange symbolizes fruitfulness, cheerfulness, earth, autumn, warmth, and richness. Green symbolizes visibility, growth, steadiness, thoughtfulness, freshness, healing, peace, and the divine.

Scriptures

For you, O Lord, are my hope, my trust, O LORD, from my youth. (Ps. 71:5)

This day shall be a day of remembrance for you. You shall celebrate it as a festival to the LORD; throughout your generations you shall observe it as a perpetual ordinance. (Exod. 12:14)

And can any of you by worrying add a single hour to your span of life? And why do you worry about clothing? Consider the lilies of the field, how they grow; they neither toil nor spin, yet I tell you, even Solomon in all his glory was not clothed like one of these. (Matt. 6:27-29)

"In the last days it will be, God declares, that I will pour out my Spirit upon all flesh, and your sons and your daughters shall prophesy, and your young [ones] shall see visions, and your old [ones] shall dream dreams." (Acts 2:17)

Poem of Reflection

CHILDREN/YOUTH: GIFTS IN TRANSITION

Our babies, gifts, jewels
Of untold, immeasurable value;
These beautiful souls, given us by God
So creative, wonderful lights
In our lives, in the world
Magnificent buds, blooming
Growing, changing
Dancing, playing, being
Wonderment, joyful
Our children, our youth
Moving through these portals
Of life itself.

Once infants and toddlers
These beautiful creatures of God
More magnificent than the lilies of the valley
Than roses in bloom
Than exquisite birds strutting about:
Our beloveds
Our offspring
Are blessed, are marvelous
And we are called to love and cherish them;
To stand witness as they experience
A rite of passage.

This ritual
Resplendent with joy and thanksgiving
An occasion of commemoration
To mark their journey
A heightened time of awareness
And new beginnings
Wherein God has a greater call on
our children and ourselves.

AN APPRECIATION DAY FOR THE PASTOR

Occasion

God calls all of us to engage in ministry. God has called some men and women, like Moses and Miriam, Priscilla and Aquila, Martin and Coretta to a ministry of leadership of the larger community of the church. God has called our own *[name of pastor and name of spouse/partner, where appropriate]* to lead, guide, and serve the community of faith. The pastor has the anointing of the Holy Spirit to preach the gospel, to teach, by precept and example, the faith principles that allow us to love God, ourselves, and our neighbors, and to go out and help bring lost souls to Christ, to set the captive free. The pastor is a teacher/learner who continues to grow in grace and mercy, as the shepherd of this flock, the body of Christ known as [name of the church]. Today we honor our shepherd, our pastor.

In joy, we thank God for the opportunity to praise and to work in covenant with our pastor in [name of the city or town]. We celebrate the gift of life and the mercy and justice of God, that God cares for us, loves us, and calls us to serve. In a spirit of humility and anticipation, we honor our pastor [and spouse/partner] for [her, his, their] dedication and commitment to God, to [name of church] family, to our community, and the world. We honor the service and accomplishments of our pastoral leadership, and bless God for blessing us with such a dynamic and priestly presence. As we celebrate today, we stand on our faith, praying for the wisdom of God, that we as pastor and faith community, may work together in harmony to share the loving, peace-based, spirit-filled message of Jesus Christ.

Welcome

To the pastor [and spouse/partner, family], officers, members of [name of church], the [name of city] community, visitors, friends: We welcome and greet you in the blessed name of Christ Jesus on the occasion of our pastor's appreciation. Today we are excited to honor the ministry, gifts, and graces of our pastor. We honor our pastor for who [he or she] is, what [he or she] does, and, most important, for [his or her] willingness to obey God's call to serve. In gratitude and appreciation, we stand in this holy place, in this sanctuary consecrated for the worship of God, welcoming you, as we anticipate that all will be blessed and renewed through your presence and participation in this service.

Our leaders are our shepherds, our guides. They motivate us to embrace life as gift and to follow the path that God sets out before us, one of loving relationships. As mentor, our pastor blesses us with care and concern, offering hope and support during difficult times. As priest, our pastor is the chief celebrant during worship and ministers to us the rites of the church. As prophet, our pastor is the vessel for the proclamation of God's word. As pastor, our minister motivates and teaches us of the faith, of tradition, and of God. We welcome you today to truly honor the ministry of our pastor as we also honor the call God has on our lives, and the gifts and graces of this community of Christ.

We offer our deepest thanks that you have chosen to join us today in this celebration. We offer thanks to God for the blessing of this powerful ministry. May we all come to know and embrace the call God has on all our lives, celebrating ordained and lay ministries. May this service inspire and nurture you; may you be moved to proclaim good news wherever you may be. Welcome.

Prayer

Loving God, Creator of us all, we come today to praise you and magnify you as we honor the life and ministry of one called by you to the ordained ministry of the church. You are so awesome yet so gentle, that you care about the lilies of the field, the birds in the air; you care about us, even when we fail to live up to the gifts that you have given us. We bless you for being eternal, powerful, the majestic presence who never sleeps or slumbers. We give thanks to you that you call and anoint people to your service. We thank you for the office of pastor, and for those who take the leap of faith to say, "here am I send me, send me."

We come on behalf of our pastor [name] and [his or her] family, their needs, wants, and desires. Please give our leader the wisdom to walk by faith, to be creative and imaginative, to know when to take action, and when to stand still and be quiet, waiting on you. Please help [her or him] have the peace that passes all understanding, and the courage to stand for justice and righteousness. As a church, help us embody Christlike principles as we work together, respecting our pastor and one another, fitting ourselves to feed the poor, help aid those that cannot see, and bring good news to the nation. Help our pastor be strong, yet not so invincible that *[he or she]* fails to rely on you; help us be a cooperative team, so that we can in love know how to support our pastor as well as challenge *[him or her]* when *[he or she]* is tired, stressed, or in need of assistance.

May we as pastor and congregation love and appreciate each other, being willing to grow closer to you, O God, in spirit and in truth, as we continue toward the path of higher calling.

Litany

LEADER: Creator God, author of the universe, you have designed your world, and you have called men and women to proclaim the good news and to lead your children.

PEOPLE: **We magnify your name, most holy One; we always carry your name on our lips, your love on our hearts, and support pastors called by you in our prayers.**

LEADER: Glory and honor, in the name of Jesus, through the power of the Holy Spirit, that those called by you, will honor you in life, in joy, in hope, as they serve your people.

PEOPLE: **Those called by God wear the mantle of grace as they move through good times and bad, facing that which may not be explainable, to honor God who is mighty.**

LEADER: Giving thanks for the office of pastor, we honor God for calling shepherds to guide and instruct us; we pray that our pastor has godly wisdom in living out this call.

PEOPLE: **We recognize the call to ordained ministry as part of God's divine construction for helping churches, bodies of Christ in the world, live out our call to serve a living God.**

ALL: **All glory and honor and praise to God, as we in humility, pastor and congregation together, come to worship, to praise, and then go out in the world to serve.**

Vow of Commitment

As we wait upon the Lord in this work of pastor, we experience renewed strength; we are empowered to mount upon wings like eagles, as we serve, and we run without getting weary, and we walk and not faint (Isa. 40:31), as we serve God as pastor and congregation. Called to serve, we recommit ourselves this day to the glory of God. God calls us to be present as stewards of creation. We humbly say yes each day to this ministry of life affirmation and transformation. As the gospel transforms us, we are open for our visions of ministry to be transformed. Each day we pray to recommit ourselves to do justice, love mercy, and walk humbly with God (Mic. 6:8), and thereby walk humbly with the body of Christ and with those souls who have yet to know the power of the message of the gospel.

In Christ, we walk by faith, not by sight (2 Cor. 5:7), we work to be open to God's leading and God's direction; we live in hope that each day we are better equipped to help spread the message of salvation. As pastor and congregation, we give witness to the power of preaching, prayer, baptism, and the *[Eucharist, Communion, or the Lord's Supper]* in the life of the church, in the realm of healing, for the possibility of truly living out God's rule in our daily lives. Our commitment to this ministry and leadership helps us to love our neighbor as we love ourselves. As congregation, we pledge to support the pastor in being guide, leader, and counselor in every aspect of the life of the church. As pastor, may the life you lead be the sermon that speaks for you.

Suggested Colors

Purple and red are the colors for Pastor's Appreciation Day. Purple symbolizes royalty, power, high energy, service, depth of feeling, and self-esteem. Red stands for love, living blood, emotion, strife, ardor, passion, anger, and warmth.

Scriptures

O save your people, and bless your heritage; be their shepherd [pastor], and carry them forever. (Ps. 28:9)

I will raise up shepherds [pastors] over them who will shepherd them, and they shall not fear any longer, or be dismayed, nor shall any be missing, says the LORD. *(Jer. 23:4)*

"The Spirit of the Lord is upon me, because [the Spirit] has anointed me to bring good news to the poor. . . . to proclaim release to the captives and recovery of sight to the blind, to let the oppressed go free, to proclaim the year of the Lord's favor." (Luke 4:18-19)

The gifts [Christ] gave were that some would be apostles, some prophets, some evangelists, some pastors and teachers, to equip the saints for the work of ministry, for building up the body of Christ. (Eph. 4:11-12)

Poem of Reflection

PASTOR IN CHARGE

Called by God
Appointed, and anointed
Our pastor is the shepherd of our church
Who proclaims the word, ministers to the sick and shut in
Serves as CEO of our community
And walks with us through our life journeys.

As pastor, you lead and guide
With godly wisdom and prudence
You listen well and must be patient
When you want to move ahead, and we are not ready;
In such moments,
When tension can ensue
Is the time for all to be in prayer
To be attuned to divine inspiration
To know how to be together
Amidst difference and change.

As pastor, leader, preacher, friend
We pray God's blessings on your ministry
That your wisdom will abound
That you are kind and gentle
Respecting the boundaries of others
Knowing how to engage without being obtrusive
That you can share love
Without being abusive
That you find your call by God
Noble, healing, and transforming.

DEACONS' AND STEWARDS' DAY

Occasion

For the work of Jesus Christ to go forward, we need a cadre, a group of workers willing to help shoulder the load and offer assistance to the pastor. Deacons or stewards often fit this role of helping tend to the financial and spiritual well-being of the pastor and congregants. Today we come to honor and celebrate the office of deacon or steward: persons who are followers of Christ in relationship to the Lord, to one another, and to the other congregants. *[Deacons or stewards]* help shoulder the responsibility of lay leadership, of financial development, and of providing support for the pastor. These leaders assist in providing guidance, and help direct plant operations, business activities, and provide support for the church's ongoing ministries.

The lay ministry of [deacon or steward] is a noble enterprise and central to the healthy growth of a church and the successful delegation of authority in the body of Christ. Today we honor [deacons or stewards] as those who work tirelessly to help the pastor and other officers with practical, spiritual, financial, and property matters. This office in the life of the church is one of service, authority, and responsibility. Deacons or stewards are persons of integrity called to participate in the leadership of the local church. Called to be prayerful, creative, and committed, these leaders provide invaluable service and support to the ministry of the church in the world.

We celebrate these dedicated officers in the service of the Lord, as we bless God for anointing them with the wisdom and courage to serve. We honor and cherish these leaders who not only provide guidance in matters of stewardship, but who also serve by participating in Sunday school, mission, home and hospital visitation, in choirs or on the usher board. We honor these leaders of distinction.

Welcome

Beloveds in Christ Jesus, we the pastor, officers, and members of [name of the church] welcome you today, as we celebrate the office and ministry of [deacon or steward]. We come making a joyful noise unto the Lord to praise and adore our Creator. We come giving thanks for the witness and lived testimony of those leaders who are of good repute, who are filled with the spirit of wisdom, who have been appointed to the duty of service to the church as they are devoted to the ministry of the word of God.

We are so honored that you decided to visit us today. God smiles in heaven when the faithful gather to praise and acknowledge the work of God on earth. [Deacons or stewards] are central to the work of our church, and your presence today pays tribute to their committed service. In their honor we praise God, offer songs, prayers, and extend our heartfelt hospitality to you. We come together to fellowship with one mind, one heart, one spirit. We welcome you to embrace the love of God and the power of the Holy Spirit in this sanctuary as we experience deep gratitude for life and for the service, joy, and ministry of our *[deacons or stewards]*. Please make yourselves comfortable and let us know if you have any other needs. Welcome in love; welcome in hope; welcome in joy; welcome.

Prayer

Blessed God Most High, how magnificent are you in all of the earth. You have established the world, the heavens, the moon and the stars; we give you all honor and praise as we are mindful of your greatness. This day we thank you for the office and ministry of *[deacons or stewards]*, and for their wonderful contributions to the life of *[name of the church]* and to the community of *[name of town or city]*. Just as you have given humanity dominion over the earth, you give us the opportunity to have responsibility for the church and the ministry of the gospel in trust.

We give thanks to the Lord with our minds, spirits, and hearts, as we join in community with gratitude for the opportunity to be leaders in the church of God. We thank you for being the God of liberation and hope. May we be so touched by your mercy and goodness that we too will work for justice and the liberation of all people. We pledge to be worthy stewards of all our gifts and graces, tithing our time, talents, and finances. As we trust and take refuge in the Lord, we will work to earn the trust of our congregation, that they might follow our lead. We are so honored to hold these offices in trust. We give thanks for this opportunity and joyfully accept this responsibility. Thanks be to God.

Litany

LEADER: Just as the Lord is the shepherd of us all, some of us are called to assist the shepherd in the ministry to the sheep; Dick Gregory, as a shepherd of liberation and comedy, has used humor as a weapon in the struggle of African Americans against inequity and racism.

PEOPLE: We give thanks for shepherds like Dick Gregory and Hank Aaron, who used a major league home-run record and Muhammad Ali who used the heavyweight boxing title to further the cause of equality and freedom for African Americans.

LEADER: Deacons and stewards are shepherds who work for total freedom of congregations, the freedom from sin and the freedom from discrimination.

PEOPLE: Many shepherds—artists and entertainers— across the years and particularly during the 1960s Civil Rights movement have taken time from their prestigious schedules to work for justice and freedom; by their actions, they demonstrated the call of Jesus to love the neighbor as we love God and love ourselves.

LEADER: Many African American journalists and publishers like Carl Rowan, Thomas Hamilton, William Monroe Trotter, Robert Abbott, A. Philip Randolph, Leon Washington, and John Johnson were deacons of justice as they pled the cause of justice for the oppressed and exploited.

PEOPLE: As people of faith and service, we give thanks for all persons committed to leading God's people to salvation and liberation. We honor the office of deacon and steward as those called by God to be support in the development of ministry.

ALL: **To God be the glory as we work for liberation of all peoples, as we listen for the leading of the Holy Spirit, that we might keep God's covenant, aware daily of the miracles that God has done.**

Vow of Commitment

O loving, redeeming Lord, often we have cried out to you as we hunger and thirst after your righteousness. We give thanks for the opportunity to serve you and your people as stewards and deacons of your great riches and blessings. You have delivered us and healed us so many times. In gratitude, we recommit to a ministry of leadership, caring, and covenant, as we are willing to take the authority to offer guidance and direction in the day-to-day work of the church. We are willing to be at the forefront in tithing, doing Bible study, sharing the gospel with others, and seeing that we have a strong ministry of benevolence to offer support to those who stand in need.

As shepherds working with the pastor to tend to the needs of the congregation and the community, we stand humbled by the responsibility before us. When we become weary and confused, help us focus on you, loving God, and experience renewal through the power of the Holy Spirit. We give thanks that we have a ministry to children, teens, young adults, adults, and seniors; that our ministry is inter-generational. Help us to teach by precept and example. Help us to learn daily how to grow stronger in our walk with you; to improve in our leadership skills with each opportunity to serve.

Suggested Colors

Purple and green are the colors for celebrating deacons or stewards. Purple symbolizes royalty, power, high energy, depth of feeling, and self-esteem. Green denotes steadiness, thoughtfulness, freshness, healing, peace, visibility, growth, and the divine.

Scriptures

O guard my life, and deliver me; do not let me be put to shame, for I take refuge in you. May integrity and uprightness preserve me, for I wait for you. (Ps. 25:20-21).

My words declare the uprightness of my heart, and what my lips know they speak sincerely. (Job 33:3)

[Jesus] answered, "You shall love the Lord your God with all your heart, and with all your soul, and with all your strength, and with all your mind; and your neighbor as yourself." (Luke 10:27)

Deacons likewise must be serious, not double-tongued, not indulging in much wine, not greedy for money. (1 Tim. 3:8)

Poem of Reflection

DEACONS/STEWARDS: LEADERS IN MOTION

Deacons, leaders, stewards, servants at the helm
Called by God to guide and serve
Be serious, of faith and clear conscience
Loving God, embracing ministry
Skilled in management
Strong of poise
Gentle of heart
Committed to the End.

Being of good report
Standing on the promises of God
Stewards or deacons abide in faith
Champion the cause of righteousness
Are persuaded of their responsibility
Noble in statute, courageous in heart.

With one mind, these leaders approach the throne of grace
As they prayerfully help plan the programs of the church;
With one heart, they know their cups overflow
With much love for all, as they move toward healing;
With one soul, they sing the praises of the Lord

Standing boldly for God
Marching up to Mt. Zion
Lifting voice in praise and authority
To do the work of councils and assemblies,
Following the rules, guided by the Spirit.

DEACONESSES' AND
STEWARDESSES' DAY

Occasion

Standing tall with regal air, *[deaconesses or stewardesses]* are women revered and highly respected in the church. These women stand at the portals of the faith of *[name of church]* as they have offered prayers, words of encouragement, baked cakes and cookies, visited the sick, taught Sunday school, and helped lead youth retreats. These "mothers" of the church share tons of wisdom with all who will listen. Today we gather to pay tribute to those who serve in the office of *[deaconesses or stewardesses]*: persons who are followers of Christ, in relationship with the Lord, other *[deaconesses or stewardesses]*, and to the other congregants. They possess a generosity of spirit and graciousness in demeanor.

Each day that we live is a tremendous gift. This day we celebrate as gift by taking this opportunity to remember the loving service and care of our beloved *[deaconesses or stewardesses]*. We honor *[deaconesses or stewardesses]* as those who work diligently to support the church's total ministry, and offer assistance to the pastor and other officers with practical spiritual, financial, and property matters. The lay ministry of *[deaconesses or stewardesses]* is one of service and love, central to the healthy growth of a church and the successful delegation of authority in the body of Christ. *[Deaconesses or stewardesses]* are persons of integrity called to important leadership in the local church. Called to be prayerful, creative, and committed, these gentle leaders provide invaluable service and support to the ministry of the church in the world. This office in the life of the church is one of responsibility, authority, and service.

We acknowledge these dedicated officers who daily serve the Lord, as we bless God for anointing them with the insight and boldness to serve. We bless and treasure these leaders who provide guidance in matters of benevolence, and who also serve by participating in mission, home and hospital visitation, Sunday school, in choirs or on the usher board. We thank God for their service and we offer tribute to these leaders of distinction.

Welcome

Friends and children of God, we the pastor, officers, and members of *[name of the church]* welcome you today, as we celebrate the office and ministry of *[deaconess or stewardess]*. We rejoice this day and offer praises unto God, our Creator and our Refuge. We give thanks for the lived, joyous testimony of those leaders who are of good standing, who are filled with the spirit of loving-kindness, who have been appointed to the duty of compassion and service to the church in devotion to the ministry of the word of God.

To our visitors and members, thank you so much for your presence today. As believers, we gather to worship and give witness to the work of God on earth. *[Deaconesses or stewardesses]* are vital to our church's well-being, and today we all recognize their committed service. Today, we praise God, sing, pray, and welcome all who have come to honor the *[deaconesses or stewardesses]* of *[name of church]*. How blessed we are to have you here, as we too celebrate their individual and communal gifts. We welcome you to this service, and the doors of *[name of church]* are always open to you, in the name of Jesus through the power of the Holy Spirit. We give thanks for life and for the service, joy, and ministry of our *[deaconesses or stewardesses]*. Please let us know if there is anything we can do to make you more comfortable. We welcome you in hope; welcome you in joy; welcome you in love; welcome.

Prayer

Everlasting God, we come to adore you and praise you, for you are an awesome God. We love you and humbly stand in your presence with singing, prayer, praise, and grateful hearts. You called us into being and have been Creator, Comforter, and guide for our ancestors and for us, and will be for generations to come. We give you thanks for the lives and ministries of our *[deaconesses or stewardesses],* and for their enormous support to the life of *[name of the church]* and to the community of *[name of town or city]*. In their ser-vice as they visit the sick and shut-in, as they wait on the Lord's Table—they honor their responsibilities you have given them for the church and the ministry of the gospel.

Thanks be to God for our health, strength, and sense of purpose, as we join together in community with appreciation for the opportunity to be leaders in the church of God. We praise you for being the God of possibility and deliverance. May we be so touched by your love, mercy, and justice that we too will work for the freedom and health of all people. We vow to take care of and honor all our gifts and graces, tithing our time, talents, and finances. As we lean and depend on you, we will work to earn the trust of our congregation, that they might follow our lead. We are so blessed to hold these offices, and will study to show ourselves approved. We give thanks for life and for this leadership responsibility. Thanks be to God.

Litany

LEADER: Merciful God, *El Roi,* who sees all, we rejoice at the gifts and opportunities afforded women to step in faith to shepherd others and lead like Senator Carol Mosley Braun of Illinois, and Lucie E. Campbell, who bridged the inspirational world of music between Charles Albert Tindley and Thomas A. Dorsey.

PEOPLE: **For those who have been sister shepherds in the worlds of church music and church leadership, we give thanks, notably Mahalia Jackson, Albertina Walker, Roberta Martin, Jarena Lee, Mattie E. Coleman, and Katie Cannon.**

LEADER: We rejoice for those outspoken, courageous shepherds who continue to advocate for the role of women in the church and larger society, including Nannie Helen Burroughs, Julia Foote, Cheryl Townsend Gilkes, Leontine Kelly, and Vashti McKenzie.

PEOPLE: **Like our *[deaconesses or stewardesses]*, women like Rosa Parks, Fannie Lou Hamer, Septima Clark, Lucy Parsons, Dorothy Height, Nettie Napier, and Estelle Osborne have stood for the cause of justice, have worked for better living and working conditions, and themselves are symbols of advocacy, training, and opportunity.**

LEADER: Many *[deaconesses or stewardesses]* are role models and advocates for our children; many women leaders serve similar roles in the larger world through advocacy and are writers of children's literature: Marian Wright Edelman, Charlene Hill Rollins, Lucille Clifton, Eloise Greenfield, Rosa Guy, Virginia Esther Hamilton, and Charlemae Hill Rollins.

PEOPLE: **For the women who shepherd us, as mentors, educators, entertainers, activists; for those in the professions who guide and help take care of us; for those who offer a word of prayer, and press a few dollars in our hands, we give thanks.**

ALL: **God of Grace, and God of Glory, we bless, honor, and love our *[deaconesses or stewardesses]* and commend their health, strength, and faith to your loving care.**

Vow of Commitment

O merciful, joyous God, often we have prayed mightily as we pondered our next right step. We give thanks that you are an ever-present God and that you have called us to serve as *[deaconesses or stewardesses]*. You have blessed us with insight to help others year in and year out. In thanksgiving, we acknowledge your blessings to us and your call on our lives to be in covenant relationships, to take the authority to take charge and offer direction in the daily life and work of the church. We are willing to be leaders and followers in this ministry, which exists in a concrete manner as tithing, doing Bible study, sharing the gospel with others. Grant us the gift of empathy when we do ministry of teaching, leadership, and benevolence to offer charity to our neighbors with grace.

As shepherds working in full partnership with the *[deacons or stewards]* and the pastor to help meet the needs of the congregation and the community, we stand in awe of the responsibility before us. We are so blessed to be chosen. Yet, when we become tired or misunderstood, help us focus on you, merciful God, and help us be rejuvenated through the power of the Holy Spirit. We give thanks that we share with others in our ministry to children, teens, young adults, adults, and seniors, in our intergenerational ministry. Help us grow closer to you; and improve in our capacity to lead and to serve.

Suggested Colors

Purple and pink are the colors for Deaconess or Stewardess Day. Purple symbolizes royalty, power, high energy, depth of feeling, and self-esteem. Pink (rose, fuchsia, or hot pink) denotes warmth, passion, high spirits, and welcome.

Scriptures

I have been like a portent to many, but you are my strong refuge. (Ps. 71:7)

[Solomon] said, "O LORD, God of Israel, there is no God like you, in heaven or on earth, keeping covenant in steadfast love with your servants who walk before you with all their heart." (2 Chr. 6:14)

Take my yoke upon you, and learn from me; for I am gentle and humble in heart, and you will find rest for your souls. (Matt. 11:29)

But speaking the truth in love, we must grow up in every way into [the One] who is the head, into Christ. (Eph. 4:15)

Poem of Reflection

DEACONESS/STEWARDESS: REGAL WOMEN OF HOPE

*Standing up for Jesus
Noble women of faith
Loving, caring, joyous for the Lord
In all their steps and gracious words
Rendered in ministry
Touching spirits, hearts, and minds
Of God's children
Like a Balm in Gilead
That can heal the sin-sick soul.*

*Benevolence personified
Sharing the gospel
Witnessing to lost souls;
Offering comfort,
A gentle smile, open arms
To hold one while grieving
To make cakes and tea
Bringing hospitality;
To soothe those in pain,
To listen well
To do the work of ministry.*

*Women of hope, women of peace
Noble in presence, kind of heart
Gentle of spirit
Obedient to God,
Love the people well—
These gracious, stately spirits
Majestic gifts of God.*

WOMEN'S MISSIONARY
SOCIETY DAY

Occasion

After the Resurrection, the first person who went to
the tomb and received the good news to share with others,
was a woman, Mary Magdalene.* Thus from Easter Sunday,

---

*In my reading of the New Testament, I find that each Gospel has different
details of the post-resurrection story. In Mark 16, Jesus first appears to Mary
Magdalene and she goes and tells others, who do not believe. In Matthew 28, in
the midst of an earthquake, an angel of the Lord tells Mary Magdalene and the
other Mary not to be afraid, that Jesus is risen, and they are to go and tell his disciples to meet Jesus in Galilee. In Luke 24, two men in dazzling apparel appear to
Mary Magdalene, Joanna, Mary the mother of James., and other women and tell
them that Jesus is risen, and the women left to share this news with the remaining
eleven disciples. In John 20, Mary Magdalene comes to the empty tomb, then runs
and tells Simon Peter, and the beloved disciple, then Peter comes, and the disciples return to their homes. As Mary Magdalene stands weeping, two angels
appear and ask why she is crying. When she states because you have taken away

women have been engaged in ministry, and sharing the good news of the gospel. Just as God called Mary Magdalene, Joanna, Mary the mother of James, and others to tell the good news, God calls *[name of missionary society, guild or auxiliary and church]* to go and share the good news with the community of faith and to do outreach to those who have not heard. Missionaries are to go out to minister to the sick and shut-in and to help bring lost souls to Christ. The *[Women's Missionary Society or Women's Guild or Women's Auxiliary]* have a calling on their lives to share the words of the gospel, to help evangelize, for they are God's ambassadors to those in need. Today, we honor these women of faith of *[name of church]*.

In deep joyfulness, we thank God for the opportunity to worship today and to support the ministry of the missionaries of our church in *[name of the city or town]*. We celebrate the loving-kindness and generous mercy of God, that God calls us to serve, and that we have the capacity to do so. In a spirit of faith and hope, we honor our missionary society for their tremendous service and dedication to God, to *[name of church]* family, to our community, and the world. We honor their compassionate service and accomplishments, and thank God for blessing us with such powerful, loving women *[missionaries or guild or auxiliary]*. As we celebrate today, we stand on our faith, praying for the wisdom of God, that together we can work in harmony to share the loving, redeeming, healing message of Jesus Christ.

Welcome

To the pastor, officers, members, and friends of *[name of church]*: how blessed are we this day, to come into God's

---

my Lord, she turns around and sees Jesus there. Jesus tells Mary to go and tell the others about his appearance and his impending Ascension.

holy temple, in joyous celebration, to honor and exalt God, as we welcome all of you for this momentous occasion. God has blessed the [Women's Missionary Society or Women's Guild or Women's Auxiliary] of this church and has given them tremendous gifts, calling them to excellence in a ministry of passionate caring. We welcome you. We are so honored that you have graced us with your presence. We welcome you to join us in worshiping and glorifying God. Our joy is overwhelming and our anticipation of what will unfold during this worship service is great. We have come to celebrate life, to have another opportunity to hear proclamation in word and song, as we set aside this time to acknowledge the contribution of all those who engage in mission on behalf of [name of church].

We, the [Women's Missionary Society or Women's Guild or Women's Auxiliary] of [name of church] welcome you in deep appreciation, ten times over! We thank you for being present today that we might share the message of the gospel with you, as we also honor others of African descent who have made tremendous contributions to our world in sharing the gospel, in helping educate God's people. These leaders include Phillis Wheatley, whose poems challenged the racist and paternalistic attitudes of Euro-Americans two years before the Revolutionary War; Mary McCleod Bethune, whose leadership of the National Association of Colored Women and her founding of the National Council of Negro Women had a significant impact on women's leadership, on socio-economic and moral values, and her founding of a college with $1.50 and a vision. We honor the legacy of Gwendolyn Brooks, who used her art as a black aesthetic to help the liberation of black folk; and the artistry of Katherine Dunham, who was first in researching the impact and reality of African dance throughout the world. Each of these women had a mission. We welcome you and invite you to embrace your mission, the desires and dreams God has laid on your heart with the [Women's Missionary Society or Women's Guild or *Women's Auxiliary]* of this church. Your home is our home; please avail yourselves of our hospitality. May something that you see and experience inspire you. Welcome.

Prayer

God Most High, from everlasting to everlasting, we come to this worship this day with entreating hearts, thanking you for your greatness, your consideration, your love and generous benevolence. Thank you for loving us and for forgiving us, when sometimes we are afraid to confess and love ourselves. We gather from places far and near, with different needs, wants, and experiences. Some of us coming celebrating healing, some of us are mourning deep losses. We yearn to do your will in our daily lives, and we have a deep desire to do the work of mission. We thank you for being a doctor in a sick room, a lawyer in a courtroom, and all around loving guide and mentor for all who thirst.

Help us model your love as we engage in missionary activities. Strengthen us and fit us for this journey. May this *[Women's Missionary Society or Women's Guild or Women's Auxiliary]* Day celebration embody all that is holy and gracious. Help us work with each other, not letting our differences hinder our capacity to grow, give, and serve. Help us grow stronger in faith, and shape our attitudes, our ways of being, and our hearts that we will be able to welcome others with sincerity from our local community of *[name of city or area]*. Bless us that we might be a blessing to others. Make this time together a joyous one that honors you and fortifies us for the work ahead. For the gift of life and for all other blessings, we give thanks. Amen.

Litany

LEADER: We celebrate the gifts of life and the opportunities to share with others the awesome power of God, and the difference it makes when one serves a risen Lord.

PEOPLE: **Just as the word of God is living and vital, God calls us to share this good news to set the captives free: free from sin, want, need, enslavement from any thing, person, or place.**

LEADER: As missionaries, we model this living word, as Christ dwells in us. As believers in Jesus Christ, we are justified, sanctified, made holy and new through the power of the Holy Spirit.

PEOPLE: **This day and each day that we have breath, we are to bring good news of great joy, that Jesus the Christ is alive and has redeemed us all.**

LEADER: The loving message embodied in Jesus the Christ is a message of peace and reconciliation. This message announces eternal life, in covenant with God.

PEOPLE: **As we hear the gospel, we are to live and model the gospel in everything we do, and everywhere we go.**

ALL: **We are rebels for God, who stand in loving covenant, to teach and live the gospel of covenantal love and reconciliation; a gift of life and hope; available to all.**

Vow of Commitment

God of hope and possibility, we praise you and bless you, we honor you this day. We praise you from the heights and in the highest heavens; we praise you from the earth, amid all of your natural wonders, we lift high your name over all other names (Ps. 148). In our roles as missionaries, may we have the unspeakable joy in sharing the gospel message, may we have the grace and patience to take the time to share our stories for one who needs hope, and the willingness to listen to one who is in deep pain. We accept the challenges of being missionaries, of preparing ourselves for this walk, and are grateful to all of those who got us thus far on our path in Christ Jesus.

As missionaries, we invite the anointing of the Holy Spirit, to sanction us with the strength and courage to live a spiritual life. We pray for a faith that will continue to sustain us. We honor the gift to offer a preached and prophetic word like Carolyn Knight, Claudette Copeland, or Linda Hollies. We give thanks for the legacies of Mattie E. Coleman and Nannie Helen Burroughs that advocated for the role of women in the church and larger society. For blazing a trail for voting rights, in the business world, and for being open to God's leading to be the first African American woman consecrated as bishop in the Episcopal Church, we give thanks to Barbara Harris. We give praise and honor to God for the opportunity to serve in the field of mission, of breaking new ground, of challenging old standards, of bringing the gospel to those who have yet to hear it. We cherish each opportunity we have to serve God and to lift our sisters and brothers as we climb toward the mark of the higher calling.

Suggested Colors

Pink and white are the suggested colors for Women's Missionary Society Day. Pink (rose, fuchsia, or hot pink) denotes warmth, welcome, passion, high spirits. White, a combination of the colors of the rainbow, symbolizes peace, purity, light, and illumination.

Scriptures

On the glorious splendor of your majesty, and on your wondrous works, I will meditate. The might of your awesome deeds shall be proclaimed, and I will declare your greatness. They shall celebrate the fame of your abundant goodness, and shall sing aloud of your righteousness. (Ps. 145:5-7)

Therefore the LORD *waits to be gracious to you; therefore [the Lord] will rise up to show mercy to you. For the* LORD *is a God of justice; blessed are all those who wait for [God]. (Isa. 30:18)*

And [Jesus] answered them, "Go and tell John what you have seen and heard: the blind receive their sight, the lame walk, the lepers are cleansed, the deaf hear, the dead are raised, the poor have good news brought to them." (Luke 7:22)

The whole assembly kept silence and listened to Barnabas and Paul as they told of all the signs and wonders that God had done through them among the Gentiles. (Acts 15:12)

Poem of Reflection

WOMEN'S MISSIONARY SOCIETY, WOMEN'S GUILD, OR 'WOMEN'S AUXILIARY: LIVING THE CHALLENGE DAILY

O bright and morning star,
So radiant, that when we look inside
We see the reflection of you;
In the hearts and souls of missionary women
Called by God to minister to those in need
We experience a radiance par excellence
A loving light that cannot be squelched
Even in the depths of midnight.

O gospel women
Go forth to tell the good news
Like Mary and Joanna and Martha
teach and preach and preach and teach
In season and out of season
When you feel like it; when you don't.
O noble loving followers of Christ
You are foundational to the church militant
As many of you who have gone before
Now reside in the church triumphant.

On this side of heaven
Continue to feed the hungry
For they will starve without you;
Continue to minister to the sick
For healing is slower without you;
Continue to clothe the naked
For they will be in deep need, perhaps ashamed without you;
Continue to share a scripture and utter a prayer
for those who are hurting
For you will be a blessing for them,
And them for you.

BOARD OF CHRISTIAN EDUCATION DAY

Occasion

Jesus, a rabbi, was a teacher and a learner. He taught in parables as he sought to develop the discipline, spirituality, and moral development of the disciples. The church, the body of Christ, must be rooted in education. All of the ministries and auxiliaries of the church to function well need to be yoked with the church's overall educational mission and vision. The body that has the responsibility for the congregation's educational health is the church's Board of Christian Education, in consultation with the pastoral vision. Today we come to honor this most sacred task and calling: the Christian education of God's people.

The church's Board of Christian Education includes representatives from all the other ministries of the church. The board focuses on the instruction and training of the children, youth, and adults of the congregation. This education concerns knowledge about scripture, theology, ethics, worship, and church law, along with how to apply information to living a healthy life. The members of the congregation need to understand how the church functions, where they can best utilize their gifts, and how God calls the church to function in the world. Today we acknowledge the ministry of education in the church. We particularly come to help re-energize our commitment to educational concerns being central to all programming, worship, and outreach.

Welcome

To the pastor, clergy staff, members, and visiting friends, we welcome you to this worship service as we honor the gift of study and learning. Today, we celebrate the ministry of the Board of Christian Education. We, the officers and members of *[name of church]*, graciously receive you, extending our heartfelt welcome as we come this day in gratitude. We greet you in the name of Jesus, through the awesome power of the Holy Spirit as we honor our own educators, those with a deep passion of teaching, sharing, and learning. As we gather and worship, we honor God and the tremendous gifts of creativity, prophetic imagination, and knowledge. We are so blessed to have the opportunity to recognize our educators for their faithful, loving service to *[name of church]*. Every ministry and office of our church is part of our religious educational ministry, from preaching to Sunday school, business meetings to new members classes. Sound education anointed by the Holy Spirit helps us have a healthy, religiously informed congregation. Our Christian educators help nurture and sustain the life of our church and our people, and we thank them.

We thank you for your attendance and we welcome you to experience our worship service fully as you also participate in our educational ministry. We welcome you and are so grateful to have your presence with us this day honoring our educators, our own Christian Board of Education.

Today we welcome you with joy and invite you to think of the educators who have played a meaningful role in your life, and of those who serve us today in this service. Too often we relegate Christian education to the Sunday school and Bible study, although you are central to all of our communications and wisdom concerning *[name of church]*. On behalf of our pastor, officers, and members of *[name of church]*, we open our hearts and our church home to you. Again, thank you for serving us. We trust that you will learn from us and that we will learn from you, as we extend to you our hospitality and blessings. We thank all of our educators for their witness, service, and creativity across the years. The ministry of Christian education is a powerful one. We only learn with teachers or facilitators mentoring our growth. We are grateful for the wisdom and service of you, our educators. We thank you, our educators whom we honor today. Educators of *[name of church]* you are welcome.

Prayer

Teacher of all teachers, how we adore you; how we love your mighty, creative acts, and your wonderful gifts of life, health, and imagination. We come today recognizing the marvelous opportunity we have to share the good news of your love, mercy, and concern for us through our ministry of Christian education. Sharing the good news involves the role of teaching. We invite your wisdom and divine energies as we work to develop all aspects of our educational programs in the work and ministry of the church to members and to those in our community. Help us tap into our creative, prophetic imaginations as we select literature, design curriculum, develop workshops, and seek to meet the educational and spiritual needs of our entire congregation.

Merciful, creative God, so often we fall short of our goals for we begin tasks without an overview, without a vision for the future from a holistic perspective. Help us be willing to face our strengths and our weaknesses. Let us have the willingness to work with others, without jealousy, shame, or a sense of inferiority. How healthy it is to admit what we can do and what we cannot do, or do not yet know how to do. Anoint our leaders in Christian education with a glimpse of the big picture that we may develop programs that will meet congregational needs for the twenty-first century, supporting the teaching and preaching ministry of our pastor, and following the tenets of scripture, particularly the teachings as taught in the parables of Jesus. Order our steps in our educational endeavors, that all of your children might be better prepared to follow a Christian life, and do the ministry God calls us to do.

Litany

LEADER: Teaching is essential to the transmission of knowledge; creative teaching involves offering encouragement, listening, and helping students to find themselves.

PEOPLE: **We honor the gifts of education and teaching as we remember some of the teachers in the Bible: Moses, the schools of the prophets, the apostle Paul, the students who studied with Paul, and the Great Rabbi, Jesus Christ and his disciples; pastors, evangelists, and other teachers.**

LEADER: We give thanks for the women and men, girls and boys who work in Christian education and for the education of God's children of African descent. We give thanks for the Wilberforce University, the first black school of higher learning owned and operated by African Americans, founded by the African Methodist Episcopal Church in 1856.

PEOPLE: **We give thanks for the founding of Meharry Medical College, the first black medical school in the U.S., founded by the Freedman's Aid Society of the Methodist Episcopal Church, 1876; and for Spelman College, the first college for black women in the U.S., founded by Sophia B. Packard and Harriet E. Giles in 1881.**

LEADER: We give thanks for Frederick Douglass Patterson and for his vision to establish the United Negro College Fund to help support black colleges and black students in 1944.

PEOPLE: **We give thanks for the 100-plus historically black colleges and universities in the United States, for those committed to training educators and those called to the ordained ministry of the church.**

ALL: **Together, we can make a difference; together we can bring Christian education and make general education available to the people of God. Let us go forth releasing our fears, letting go of anti-intellectualism where it resides, and welcoming an opportunity to explore our God-given creative imaginations.**

Vow of Commitment

Everlasting, bountiful God, you who rule the wind and the waters, you who designed the world and gives the gift of intelligence, we thank you for our ability to teach and learn, to share and facilitate the exchange of information. We praise and adore you for your majestic reality and for the gifts of creation. We come before your presence with thanksgiving for all that you have done, and in anticipation for that which will unfold today. In our prophetic imagination, we invite your guidance that we might better use the faculties you have so generously given us. Endow us with a passion for new knowledge about you and about all creation.

As you make a clean heart within us, give us an ever-expanding thirst for knowledge. You invite all who have thirst to come to the water (Isa. 55); we thirst deeply for new learning and new experiences. We pray that our Board of Christian Education along with our clergy leadership will have a vision of programming to meet the needs of our household of faith. We invite the deep anointing of the Holy Spirit, so that we might be open for the miracles that you wish to bring our way. We give thanks for all inventions, for the marvelous gifts of art, music, technology, science, and literature. May we be ever faithful to you in the correct appropriation of these gifts. Bless all teachers and students. Help us to be of one accord that we might know the opportunity to learn as a generous gift of the Holy Spirit.

Suggested Colors

Yellow and red are the suggested colors for celebrating the Board of Christian Education Day. Yellow suggests liveliness, animation, radiance, good cheer, wisdom, knowledge, intelligence, inspiration, and a reflection of God's glory. Red stands for love, living blood, emotion, strife, ardor, passion, anger, and warmth.

Scriptures

Teach me your way, O LORD, that I may walk in your truth; give me an undivided heart to revere your name. (Ps. 86:11)

Teach them the statutes and instructions and make known to them the way they are to go and the things they are to do. (Exod. 18:20)

Jesus went throughout Galilee, teaching in their synagogues and proclaiming the good news of the kingdom and curing every disease and every sickness among the people. (Matt. 4:23)

Let the word of Christ dwell in you richly; teach and admonish one another in all wisdom; and with gratitude in your hearts sing psalms, hymns, and spiritual songs to God. (Col. 3:16)

Poem of Reflection

BOARD OF CHRISTIAN EDUCATION: A RULE OF FAITH

Listening, loving, learning for God
Engages us in every waking moment
That we know, hear, and see
Goodness revealed throughout the world;
Time to question, time to think
Time to ruminate, contemplate
What a mighty God we serve
How much that
God truly loves us
How gifted we are because of that love
As we shout, "Glory, Hallelujah!"*

Knowledge and new ways of knowing
Don't come in a flash, nor to the lazy;
Learning and loving
Involve a desire to learn
A desire to better perfect this sacred temple
Which includes our minds within our bodies
Given us by God.

With learning, comes responsibility
The Board of Christian Education
The vehicle for discernment and gathering
Information and resources
To help proclaim the gospel
In imaginative ways,
Big ways, little ways, surprising ways.
Showing ourselves desiring
A stronger walk with God in all ways
And thus the source of our desire
For a creative, Christian education program;
The need so great, the servants so few;
Is anybody listening?

---

*Hallelujah is a contraction from the Hebrew:

Allelu = Give Praise to + *jah* = Yahweh = *Give Praise to God*

USHERS' DAY

Occasion

Today we honor those who welcome, greet, and extend the hospitality of our church to the stranger, the visitor, and each church family member each Sunday. Ushers are the ones who graciously serve in other settings with a smile, a word of assurance, with a sense of purpose, and a wealth of directions. Today, we celebrate Ushers Day. Ushers are the gatekeepers for the house, the sacred space dedicated to the worship of God. Ushers stand tall and erect in their pristine uniforms and have the gift for putting people at ease during a worship service. Ushers are aware of the pulse of the service and at a moment's notice can offer assistance—in a crisis or emergency by providing a program or fan or obtaining emergency assistance. Ushers tend to the well-being and comfort of members in a congregation and keep a watchful eye out for the rhythm of the service, and the needs of the pastor and others in charge of service. Being a gatekeeper in the House of God is no easy ministry. Sometimes the work is tedious for it demands being on one's feet for a long time. One has to pay attention and keep focused; thus one has no room for daydreaming or silent meditation. While some of those coming to church may feel irritable and may be brusque, even disrespectful in their speech and manner, ushers always act out of professional decorum and warm hospitality. The usher provides the first impression of a church that a visitor will experience. Ushers understand the layout of the church, know where programs are to occur, and show up ahead of time to be there on time for the service itself. An usher has the opportunity to be the good Samaritan, one who extends hospitality graciously. Ushers make each of us feel welcome and feel good about ourselves. Let us celebrate ushers this day with the same joy and zeal they share with us each week as they greet us, in the Name of Jesus.

Welcome

Faithful members of the body of Christ, we welcome you to this wonderful celebration of Ushers. We, the members of *[name of church]*, greet you, extending our warmest possible hospitality as we come this day in thanksgiving. We greet you in the name of Jesus, through the awesome power of the Holy Spirit as we honor our own doorkeepers, doorkeepers for the Lord, our ushers. As we worship through song, prayer, and preaching, we honor God and all the magnificent blessings God has bestowed upon us. We are so grateful to have the opportunity to recognize our ushers, for their untiring, faithful service to *[name of church]*. Many ministries in the church are so important for the well-being of our congregation. Our ushers play a significant role in the life of our church, and we thank them so much, as we welcome you to experience our worship service fully as we honor our ushers today. As you think back on the many worship experiences you have known, think about the ones who greeted you with all sincerity and love. We welcome you and are so grateful to have your presence with us this day honoring our gatekeepers.

Today we welcome you with gladness and invite you to think of the ushers who serve us today, and to those who have gone on before. On behalf of our pastor, officers, and members of [name of church], we open our hearts and our church home to you. What an honor for us to be graced with your presence, as we extend to you our hospitality and blessings of appreciation. We cannot thank you enough for your attendance; we cannot thank our ushers enough for all of their service across the years. With their gracious manners and their warm smiles, our ushers stand as a beacon of light and hope to the stranger who comes to the door; they stand as a friend and sense of the familiar when members come to the door. As you continue to let your light so shine before all persons to the glory of God, know that you represent the presence of Christ. We are grateful for the service and support of our ushers, and again, we thank you for visiting with us and honoring our ushers with your time and presence. Friends in Christ, you are welcome.

Prayer

God who watches and waits, God who travels with us in the clouds hovering and protecting, we worship you and magnify you because you are God. We praise your awesome being in the world, on earth and in heaven. We give thanks for the many ministries you have allowed us to create as we worship and adore you. Thank you for the gifts of ushers, for their willingness to serve, to stand watch and at attention. We thank you that they are willing to face crises and to meet the smallest need during our worship services. Please bless our ushers, as they are a blessing to all who come within. Help soothe their feet when they get tired; help soften the blow when someone is unkind to them. Please give them a renewed sense of purpose and help them to take even greater delight in serving those who come into the household of faith.

Help us all love and respect our ushers in a way that honors you and blesses them. When there is a lack of clarity or confusion, please give our ushers a focus and purpose. Help them follow protocol, and help us be aware of the boundaries of place and space in the sanctuary. In so doing, let us never cause anyone discomfort or turn anyone away. Please continue to order their steps with gentleness and a sense of call and gift. We are so grateful for their gentle demeanor and regal stature. We thank them for every ceremony where they have served, and served well. Continue to bless us all to have that Christlike spirit of hospitality, where no one ever feels like a stranger and all will feel welcome.

Litany

LEADER: As Joseph provided the way for his father and brothers to be ushered into Egypt and Moses helped usher the children of Israel out of Egypt toward freedom, we are grateful for the ushers who walk with us into our journey of worship.

PEOPLE: **As Whitney Young, Jr., helped usher in economic opportunities for African Americans and Mary Church Terrell helped usher in the organizing of the National Association of Colored Women, ushers in churches accompany, support, and serve with dignity.**

LEADER: As Charles Hamilton Houston helped engineer the legal quest for equality and justice for African Americans after the reconstruction and Harriet Tubman helped conduct many slaves from bondage to freedom, ushers help orchestrate the movement of the congregation throughout the service.

PEOPLE: **As Martin R. Delaney led the movement of Black Nationalism in the United States, and scientist and inventor Benjamin Banneker, also a mathematician, astronomer, surveyor, and writer, championed the cause of enslaved blacks against the government, ushers help maintain order and decorum in the sanctuary.**

LEADER: We give thanks for the ushers who serve tirelessly during worship services, providing direction, seating, programs, and the gentle smiles and compassionate spirits that greet us at the door of the sanctuary.

PEOPLE: **Standing regally at their posts, ushers stand at the doors, as gatekeepers and greeters to let all know they are welcome in God's house. For such affirmation and loving concern, we give thanks.**

ALL: **In gratitude and thanksgiving, we honor all ushers. We acknowledge their service and abilities to show hospitality. We pray that as a congregation, we will not take their generosity for granted, that we will remember to acknowledge their gifts of presence.**

Vow of Commitment

As we joyously celebrate the office and the ministry of ushers, we give thanks for the opportunity to serve at the portals of the sanctuary, being a welcoming presence for all who enter. This day we recommit ourselves to a ministry of hospitable service, where we take joy and great delight in being doorkeepers for God. We recognize the honor it is to serve in God's house, an honor to be God's representative when the stranger or the church family member comes to the house of worship. We stand tall and proud of this commitment. We are so blessed to have this opportunity, not with false pride or arrogance, but with the pride of joy that comes from having occasions when we can give witness to the gospel because of how we help direct people regarding their roles and actions in the worship service.

We vow to continue to hone our skills so that we may be the best possible stewards of our gifts as we serve in the sanctuary. Tall will we stand as gatekeepers, that we reflect the strength and grace of the Lord. Gentle of speech will we be, so that the kindness we share will demonstrate the love of Christ Jesus to all who enter. Gracious of manner will we be, so that one needing comfort will find it in us. Wise in the programming and order of the worship service will we be, so that we can provide clarity and directions providing hospitality. Today, we recommit ourselves to the ministry of being gatekeepers for God's people.

Suggested Colors

Colors for Ushers Day celebration are orange and blue. Orange symbolizes the earth, autumn, warmth, fruitfulness, cheerfulness, and richness. Blue suggests peace, serenity, calm, work, space, royalty, and tends to be a unifying, healing element.

Scriptures

I would rather be a doorkeeper in the house of my God than live in the tents of wickedness. (Ps. 84:10b)

For the four chief gatekeepers, . . . were in charge of the chambers and the treasures of the house of God. (1 Chr. 9:26)

Whoever serves me, must follow me, and where I am, there will my servant be also. (John 12:26a)

Do not neglect to show hospitality to strangers, for by doing that some have entertained angels without knowing it. (Heb. 13:2)

Poem of Reflection

USHERS: BEACONS OF LIGHT AND HOPE

Gentle of spirit, and regal of step
Ushers offer a concrete view
Of God's rule on earth
As they welcome all
Into holy places, holy spaces
Places consecrated for the worship of God.

As arbiters of hospitality
These angels stand by the door and watch
Opening doors and greeting strangers,
Greeting families and friends
With warmth and compassion
For all are welcomed within
And if not, then the holy place
Has ceased to be the consecrated space
Of hope, love, possibility, and good news.

These angels of mercy,
With one smile and a few tender words,
Offer a sense of renewal and respite
In standing near the door,
As gatekeepers who embody
The words of Isaiah:
"Ho, everyone who has thirst, come to the water."
The water of community and concern
Of hope and transformation
Of preached, prayed, and sung word
Of encouragement and renewal;
All made plain in the smile and gentle touch
Of our angels of mercy at the door: our ushers.

MARTIN LUTHER KING, JR. DAY

Occasion

Today we celebrate a Nobel Prize winner, a martyr, a drum major for justice, a husband, father, friend, scholar, author, a black preacher, a black preacher's kid, a grand-baby of a black preacher, a son of the South: the Reverend Dr. Martin Luther King, Jr.* We honor one who pledged his life to work for social, economic, and political justice not just for African Americans, but for all people. Persuaded by the thought of Mohandas Gandhi (called the Mohatma,

---

* See Marvin McMickle, *An Encyclopedia of African American Christian Heritage* (Valley Forge, Pa.: Judson Press, 2002), 152-54; Columbus Salley, *The Black 100: A Ranking of the Most Influential African-Americans, Past and Present* (New York: Citadel Press, 1993), 3-8.

which means "Great Souled", by the common people), and observing the nonviolent struggles for independence in India, King embraced nonviolent protest, despite the violent attacks on himself and his family. He had the gift of bringing town and gown together, for rallying people from all walks of life before the language of multiculturalism was popular, for the good of all humanity. Dr. King preached a gospel of freedom, and boldly challenged others to face the responsibility of what it means to be free. On August 28, 1963, standing before the Lincoln Memorial in Washington, D.C., King gave his testament of hope and quintessential dream for equality in the United States, in his "I Have a Dream" speech.

This third-generation Baptist preacher met the ugliness of racism in many ways, early on, when he had to give up his seat to a white passenger and ride ninety miles standing in the aisle, after having won an oratory contest. In addition to helping lead sit-ins, boycotts, and marches throughout the South and the North, King and other colleagues planned and orchestrated the Southern Christian Leadership Conference (SCLC). This drum major for justice stressed the message of Jesus, "Love your neighbor," as he pressed the United States to grant its citizens of African descent their constitutional and God-given rights. Because of the protest of thousands, given voice through the magnificent rhetoric of Dr. King, Congress passed the Twenty-fourth Amendment, which removed poll taxes for voting in federal elections, and the 1965 Voting Rights Act, which revoked the use of literacy tests and other random barriers to voting by Blacks and other poor citizens. This celebration commemorates the commitment of Dr. King to global justice, indicated in his stance against the United States' participation in the Vietnam War. We honor one who wanted us to remember him, not for his awards, his popularity, or his educational degrees, but for his efforts to love and serve humanity.

Welcome

To the pastor, officers, members, and friends of [name of church]: we stand today in memoriam, as we commemorate the life of the Reverend Dr. Martin Luther King, Jr., and for all of the saints who have protested against oppression, inequality, and injustice. We come to honor and glorify God, in gratitude for the legacy and life of Dr. King, as we welcome each one of you for this momentous, historic occasion. As we come together today, we invite you to recall the various aspects of his ministry, and remember his family who lost a husband and a father to the assassin's bullet at age thirty-nine. We welcome you to celebrate this national holiday and to reflect on how we can stand for justice today.

Knowing that you could have visited many other churches today, we thank you for choosing to worship and fellowship with us. Let us lift our voices with strength and fervor just as men and women, boys and girls sang behind bars when they were jailed for protesting injustice, and were treated worse than second-class citizens. We lift our voices in prayer, grateful for where we have come from, and committed to make an even greater difference in the present and future for civil rights. We welcome you to participate in our service and to tell others about your blessed experience with us. Thank you for being with us today. You honor us by being here. Welcome friends, for all are welcomed in the house of God. Welcome, welcome, welcome.

Prayer

God of love, mercy, and justice, how noble, blessed, and kind you are. In gratitude, we celebrate the life and legacy of the Reverend Dr. Martin Luther King, Jr., who followed the call to serve and love given us by Jesus the Christ. We thank you for his life, his commitment, and passion for you and for justice. How he honored the words of Micah as he did what you required of him: loved mercy, did justice, and walked humbly with you. May we, like him, "have the strength to love," and not let our ignorance and fear keep us from loving others who are different from us. May we embody the truest tenets of our Christian faith, as we open ourselves to becoming more Christlike, helping us walk the walk and talk the talk with people from all arenas of life.

When we have our "kitchen table experiences at midnight," when we are so forlorn that we can think of no way out, help us remember all of the prophets and ambassadors for justice, like Dr. King. Many of them have also sat at the table and wept, but when they stood up, they stood up empowered, they stood up knowing your "amazing grace," experiencing the power of your mercy and love. Help us honor your call to do justice. Let us not fret or worry over the realities of violence, but recommit ourselves to work for peace. Help us work at home, at church, and in larger society for the day when our children, when all of us will be assessed by the content of our character not by the color of our skin, our class, our gender, our credentials, or who we know. We offer these prayers in thanksgiving and in hope for the breakthrough within us and within society that will let freedom ring.

Litany

LEADER: You have called us to dream dreams and have visions of equality and justice, throughout the world. Help us be visionaries for the gospel of justice and righteousness.

PEOPLE: **As we embrace the gospel of justice and righteousness, we embrace the call and responsibility of freedom, freedom to be the magnificent persons God called into being.**

LEADER: We stand for freedom for all of God's children; to be Black, White, Red, Brown, and Yellow together; we pray for justice for humanity everywhere; we vow to work for peace, within ourselves, at home and abroad.

PEOPLE: **Because violence is wrong on the streets of the United States, violence is wrong everywhere. May our world leaders be empowered to orchestrate a world that thrives on cooperation and peace, not on competition and greed.**

LEADER: The struggle for the lived gospel of Jesus Christ is a struggle for human rights; may we stand steadfast on the laws of love: love the Lord your God with all your heart, and love your neighbor as yourself.

PEOPLE: **In the spirit of the Montgomery bus boycott and Dr. King's "Letter from a Birmingham Jail," we make our manifesto this day, as a call for justice and freedom now.**

ALL: **Through the grace of God and the power of nonviolent witness, in anticipation we sing, "Free at last, free at last, thank God Almighty, we're free at last."**

Vow of Commitment

We stand today in the legacy of the Reverend Dr. Martin Luther King, Jr. and the hundreds of thousands of foot soldiers for justice, as we recommit to the freedom of all people, everywhere. We honor the legacy of all of God's drum majors for justice and righteousness. We recall Dr. King's reminder for us to work for a beloved community, by daily seeking to see "If we can help somebody," as we pass through this life. As Christians and justice seekers, we cannot merely speak the words and offer platitudes in moments of duress; we must connect action with our thinking and being. As we work for justice in the world, it is critical for us to work for justice at home. We desire to participate fully as citizens of faith, embracing nonviolent direct protest.

As we "stride toward freedom," we humble ourselves before God that we might discern when, where, and how we are called to function. We know that the cause of freedom is ever before us. We pledge to practice a life of freedom, where we do not become slaves to any ideas or ways of being, as individuals or as communities. We invite the anointing of the Holy Spirit to open up our creative imaginations in ways that will help us live a life of justice in community; that will help us not become idolatrous to ideas and actions that fly in the face of freedom and justice for all. We stand with our sisters and brothers who daily fight against any forms of oppression, that stifle their access to freedom—denying their creativity, their being, their very souls.

We have a dream, and we share it with all: We shall not be moved from this dream.

Suggested Colors

Black, white, and red are the colors for celebrating the life and legacy of the Reverend Dr. Martin Luther King. Black symbolizes solidarity, strength, power, and infinity. White, a combination of the colors of the rainbow, symbolizes peace, purity, light, and illumination. Red symbolizes love, passion, grandeur, life, courage, and living blood.

Scriptures

Give justice to the weak and the orphan; maintain the right of the lowly and the destitute. Rescue the weak and the needy; deliver them from the hand of the wicked. (Ps. 82:3-4)

What does the LORD require of you but to do justice, and to love kindness, and to walk humbly with your God? (Mic. 6:8b)

Every valley shall be filled, and every mountain and hill shall be made low, and the crooked shall be made straight, and the rough ways made smooth; and all flesh shall see the salvation of God. (Luke 3:5-6)

The tribune answered, "It cost me a large sum of money to get my citizenship." Paul said, "But I was born a citizen." (Acts 22:28)

Poem of Reflection

MARTIN LUTHER KING, JR.: PROPHET OF JUSTICE

Noble one, called by God
Born in a Baptist parsonage
Brilliant and erudite in academics
Passionate and powerful in the pulpit
Lover of life and of people
So awesome are you
The U.S. government dubbed a day
Honoring you,
One who honored the call of God
And the great need of a hurting, oppressed people.

Resplendent in your oratory and prayers
Nudging the faith of the folk
As they put life and hope on the lines,
To protest against the injustice:
The stolen freedoms, and gifts of citizenship
From a people, who made it over
The ocean, and slavery
To be shackled and lynched by Jim Crow
Solely based on the color of their skin.
How hard this was for them
How painful was this, is this for God.

Drum major for justice:
You strode regally before hundreds
Spiritually and actually
As hundreds walked miles to work
Hundreds protest segregated public accommodations
Hundreds faced death and crossed the Edmund Pettus Bridge
Thousands sat in the lap of Abraham Lincoln,
as you forecast the dream;
All celebrated when you received the Nobel Prize
Millions mourned your death;
And yet the prophets of God
Are often bigger in death, than life;
Thank you for being a dreamer
For being a drum major for justice
For following the call of God.

WATCH NIGHT

Occasion

On this night before God ushers in a new year, we gather in the tradition of the original watch-night services, Methodist prayer services that began spontaneously at Kingswood, England, April 1742. Some converted miners gathered and spent much of the evening in prayer and praise, as they tried to stay out of trouble. When some wanted John Wesley, the founder of Methodism, to stop these services, he stated that this practice had roots in ancient Christianity and he refused to forbid the vigil. The first watch-night services held in North America occurred at St. George's parish, Philadelphia, and at Wesley Chapel, New York City, in November 1770.*

---

* See http://www.greenspun.com/bboard/q-and-a-fetch-msg.tcl?msg id=00BgLB; Charyn D. Sutton, "Watch Night," The Onyx Group, December 2000; http://www.onyx-group.com/WatchNight.htm.

The roots for *African American Watch Night Services*, also known as "Freedom's Eve," that we celebrate this evening, began December 31, 1862. African Americans gathered in churches and private homes throughout the United States as they anxiously waited to hear that the Emancipation Proclamation had become federal law. According to President Abraham Lincoln's promise, all slaves in the Confederate States were legally free at the stroke of midnight, January 1, 1863. These newly freed people responded with prayers, shouts, and songs of gratitude and joy. Tonight we stand in that tradition and give thanks for these rich legacies of standing in watch for the New Year, for renewal, for new beginnings. May all that we do here reverberate through the years, linking with those who have gone before and those who will come in the future.

Welcome

On this 365th evening of *[date of the present year]*, we stand on the mountaintop looking over into the New Year of *[date of the new year]* with gratitude and thanksgiving. In anticipation and joy, we, the pastor, officers, and members of *[name of church]*, welcome you with open hearts to this Watch Night celebration. We gather in this vigil to focus on the blessings of the past year, and we pray to be in the mind of God as we launch into the New Year. We are overjoyed that, of all the places you could have been this evening, you have come to this sacred place, this sanctuary to worship God. We invite you to join us as we focus on God and the profound ways in which God has blessed us to see another year. We invite you to participate fully in this service of thanksgiving, that you might experience a powerful connection with God Almighty, and with the saints of Christ gathered here.

By celebrating this New Year together in worship, we resolve this evening to refocus our lives on God. Together we have come to watch the ringing out of the old year and the ringing in of the new. As watchers of the night, we invite you to pray that this year might bring more peace to the world, our loved ones, our society, and ourselves. As we watch the New Year come in, we invite you to think about how far you have come in a year. We celebrate our freedom that people have fought and died for, that we might be grateful for the gifts of liberty, access, accountability, and opportunity. As we watch tonight, we can remember our anticipation of this New Year, and bring that same kind of anticipation to each day. Then each day becomes an opportunity for us to wait on the Lord, and to watch each day for God's call on our lives; that is, how we do ministry. We invite you to think about who you are and whose you are in this grand moment of anticipation. We welcome you to this watch night service and to a year of watching with anticipation of deliverance. Welcome, welcome; Happy New Year.

Prayer

Eternal God of our blessed years, God of our hopes, who holds our tears, we come in thanksgiving and anticipation to bless and praise you for the gift of another year. Just as you had the shepherds watch by night at the birth of Jesus the Christ, we watch with all the company of heaven and our ancestral cloud of witnesses, as we greet the New Year. As we watch, we adore and worship you. As we watch, please touch our hearts, our bodies, and our minds, that we may be more loving stewards of all the gifts and graces you have bestowed upon us. Help us love you before all others. Bless us that we might learn to love ourselves and treat ourselves as the holy beings you created us to be when you pronounced us as made in your image, and made good.

As we greet this New Year, help us watch how we treat one another. May we confess the good and the bad that we have done, and the good and bad that have been done to us:

first naming the wrong and the pain. When we have fully faced these wrongs, help us begin the process of forgiving ourselves. Help us place on the altar those things that we need to forgive ourselves for, and all of those persons we need to forgive who have done us wrong. As we forgive, help us learn from these situations, that we may watch with deep insight, so that we do not repeat our mistakes about what we do and whom we trust. Help us watch wisely and wait on you, for our renewal, our strength, that we may better serve you, and honor your light in our lives.

Litany

LEADER: We gather for this vigil, as a community, to greet the New Year in prayer and praise; in gratitude and hope as a covenant of grace.

PEOPLE: **With this covenant of grace, we accept God's invitation to renewed obedience to Christ; that as Christians, we vow to be more Christ-like in thought and deed.**

LEADER: Like Adam Clayton Powell, Sr., Adam Clayton Powell, Jr., Samuel Proctor, and Calvin O. Butts III have held the watch at the historic Abyssinian Baptist Church and been engaged in the socioeconomic and political development of Harlem, we stand watch here in our community, committed to serve the church and society.

PEOPLE: **This year, we commit to stand watch over our personal growth and the development of our church and community, for the enrichment of God's gifts to us, including the gift of freedom.**

LEADER: We give thanks for those who have kept watch over the thought and actions of nonviolence and passive resistance to help nurture our cause for civil rights, including the Reverend James Lawson, Fannie Lou Hamer, Bayard Rustin, Septima Clark, Rev. Fred Shuttlesworth, Bernice Johnson Reagon, Ella Baker, and Jo Ann Robinson.

PEOPLE: **As a new day and the new year dawns, we give thanks for those who have worked for freedom and justice. We pledge to continue to keep watch for ourselves and for our community, in the quest for freedom from injustice, and freedom from sin.**

ALL: **As the old year ends and the New Year comes in, we stand together as community in gratitude for what God has done and for what God will do in our lives this new year.**

Vow of Commitment

This evening on the eve of a New Year, we recommit ourselves to our lives with Christ: a life of compassion, community-building, and caring for our children, youth, young adults, and adults. Standing watch as stewards of God's creation and God's church, we are blessed by God's tremendous generosity and know that with these gifts comes a great deal of responsibility. In the name of Jesus, through the power of the Holy Spirit, we stand to renew the vows we made to the Lord during our baptism. As we launch into a New Year, we are open to God's call and leading. We pledge to embrace the preached word, to teach through our lived example, and to listen for the majestic beauty of God in all creation.

As we glimpse into the New Year, we fret not about the past, nor will we obsess about the future. We pray to learn from our past mistakes and to have an attitude of gratitude in the present that we might fully experience God's grace, moment by moment. Knowing that God will never leave us or forsake us, we will work to live each day as it comes, knowing that we are building on the past and building for the future, by God's grace, not worrying about either. With the gift of the New Year is another opportunity for us to be the eyes and ears of God, for us to watch for those who yet need to hear the words of love and salvation and to listen that we might learn how to minister in each unique situation. With this Watch Night service, we praise and glorify the God of past, present, and future, so blessed to be alive to see another year.

Suggested Colors

Suggested colors for Watch Night are yellow and red. Yellow suggests liveliness, animation, radiance, good cheer, wisdom, knowledge, intelligence, inspiration, and a reflection of God's glory. Red symbolizes grandeur, life, courage, love, passion, and living blood.

Scriptures

I will instruct you and teach you the way you should go; I will counsel you with my eye upon you. (Ps. 32:8)

You have granted me life and steadfast love, and your care has preserved my spirit. (Job 10:12)

Beware of false prophets, who come to you in sheep's clothing but inwardly are ravenous wolves. (Matt. 7:15)

Devote yourselves to prayer, keeping alert in it with thanksgiving. (Col. 4:2)

Poem of Reflection

WATCH NIGHT: REFLECTING, PRAYING FORWARD

Between evening and midnight
Before the dawn of a new day
We watch by night
Awaiting the coming of a year
Never experienced before;
Of time untested, unborn
Due to burst forth in moments
As we pray and wait
On the Lord,
As we experience renewal of courage;
Yes, we wait on God.

Standing watch by night
Before the break of day
Time for reflecting
Giving thanks, breathing deeply
By God's grace, we did get over
The damage we did in the year past
We pray we didn't do too much harm;
We ask forgiveness for the wrongs we committed
Praying for healing of ourselves and those we wronged.
Reflecting, looking back, in gratitude.

Praying forward, we stand on the firm foundation
Of the loving mercy of God
Gifted to yet be alive,
Gifted to have an opportunity to serve
In hope, faith, and anticipation,
We have traversed mountains and valleys
To stand on the brink of today:
Happy New Year.

KWANZAA

Occasion

Today we join millions throughout the world in celebrating Kwanzaa (QUAN-ZUH), celebrated from December 26 through January 1, an African American and Pan-African holiday that celebrates family, community, and culture. Created in 1966, in the midst of the black freedom movement, by Dr. Maulana Karenga, professor and chair of the Department of Black Studies at California State University, Long Beach, Kwanzaa is a Swahili term derived from the phrase *"matunda ya kwanza"* (MA-TOON-DAH YAH QUAN-ZUH) which means "first fruits." This cultural holiday celebrates revitalization and the rich cultural legacies of Africa and peoples of the African diaspora. Kwanzaa is a process of recovery as we learn of our history and reconstruction as we build each other up in community.* Kwanzaa has Seven Principles, *Nguzo Saba* **(EN-GOO-ZO SAH-BAH)**, and seven symbols and two supplemental ones. These seven communitarian African values are: *Umoja* **(OO-MO-JAH)**, Unity; *Kujichagulia* **(KOO-GEE-CHA-GOO-LEE-YAH)**, Self-Determination; *Ujima* **(OO-GEE-MAH)**, Collective Work and Responsibility; *Ujamaa* **(OO-JAH-MAH)**, Cooperative Economics; *Nia* **(NEE-YAH)**, Purpose; *Kuumba* **(KOO-OOM-BAH)**, Creativity; and *Imani* **(EE-MAH-NEE)**, Faith. The seven symbols are *Mazao* **(MAH-ZAH-OW**, The Crops), *Mkeka* **(M-KAY-KAH**, The Mat), *Kinara* **(KE-NAH-RAH**, The Candle Holder), *Muhindi* **(MOO-HEN-DE**, The Corn), *Mishumaa Saba* **(ME-SHOO-MAAH-SAH-BAH**, The Seven Candles), *Kikombe cha Umoja* **(KE-KOM-BAH CHAH OO-MO-JAH**, The Unity Cup), and *Zawadi* **(ZAH-WAH-DEE**, The Gifts).

Kwanzaa is a time to honor integrity, beauty, and remembrance. Honoring integrity, we will not mix these values with other symbols, values, or practices. Honoring beauty, we take our time to plan our time together and create the most attractive items and gifts to be used in our celebration. Honoring remembrance, we take the time to reflect on our ancestors, our history, ourselves, and our future, emphasizing our culture and heritage in thanksgiving.

Welcome

To the pastor, officers, members, visiting friends, and all elders present this joyful day, we welcome you to [*name of*

---

* For more detailed information on Kwanzaa, please see: *Kwanzaa: A Celebration of Family, Community and Culture, Commemorative Edition,* Maulana Karenga, 1998, Los Angeles: University of Sankore Press. Source for this special day is http://www.officialkwanzaawebsite.org.

church] as we give tribute to our heritage, honor our ancestors, and celebrate our rich legacy hewn in the land of Africa, transported here with us through the Middle Passage. Today we celebrate Kwanzaa, and we are so blessed to have you as we celebrate family, culture, and community. From the earliest times in the great kingdoms of Egypt and Nubia, through the historic liberation struggles when African nations threw off the shackles of colonialism, to this historic moment, we welcome you as we honor the gifts of firstfruits.

Like those on the continent of Africa, we welcome you to share a time of ingathering, a time when we renew and reclaim our connections, our relationships of community. We welcome you this day for a time of quiet dignity and extraordinary reverence for God, our creator and for all creation; how good and wonderful creation has been to us—the food of the earth, the beauty of the skies, the bounty of the sea. We welcome you to come join with us in commemorating our historical past, so that we might learn of our great heritage as they modeled great genius and intellect long before us. We welcome you to a time of renewal and recommitment to being the best and most creative that we can be in thought, word, and deed. And we welcome you for this sacred time of celebrating that which is good all around and in us; that we see the good in the phenomenal and the simple; in the divine, in nature, in society. Welcome, welcome, welcome.

Prayer

Most Holy Creator, giver of firstfruits, life, health, strength, food, family, community, and culture, how noble and gracious are you. We revere and honor you for your many gifts and graces. We celebrate all that is holy and give thanks for the totality of our lives, our health, our strength, and our phenomenal heritage. You have been with us from time immemorial. You held our ancestral parents in your arms as they held on for life in crossing middle passage. You placed the North Star, the Drinking Gourd, in the heavens to guide our people out of slavery. You were the cloud by day and the stars by night that led many of our relatives to points North, East, and West; many of us have returned to the homes of our parents in the South. For these firstfruits and for this time of ingathering, we give thanks.

We pray for unity in our homes and faith communities, at work and at play, as we continue to strive toward freedom and let our lights so shine that others will glorify you. We ask your guidance as we embrace the gift of self-determination, that we can stand together; using the talents and creativity you have given us to speak for ourselves. We rejoice in the possibility for collective work and responsibility; for together we can do all things through Christ Jesus who strengthens us. Help us not to fear the opportunities we have to practice cooperative economics. Help us to be about business and less the victims of consumerism. We bless you, O Creator, as you call us to a purpose for ourselves and for our communities. We are so grateful for our many gifts of creativity, where we have the capacity to help build and make new things in ways we have never dreamed. And, in all things let us embrace our faith, having the capacity to overcome and build trusts with our communities, elders, teachers, and leaders, as we move forward to better embrace your love here on earth. For all of the gifts of firstfruits, we give thanks and praise.

Litany

LEADER: Oh beautiful day, oh day of joy and celebration; we honor the gift and place of unity in our communities and in our hearts.

PEOPLE: The gift of unity, as we stand together, allows us to embrace the opportunity for self-determination, where like Ruth, your people will be my people, your God, my God; for blessed by God, together we stand and speak for ourselves.

LEADER: Rebuking all chaos and backbiting, we acknowledge our desire to help build up our community and our commitment to work together to help each other solve our problems.

PEOPLE: Looking forward on this day, we embrace cooperative economics as a way to help sustain our communities and improve the present for our children's future.

LEADER: As we dream dreams and rethink the nature of our communities, we accept the challenge to be purposeful in focusing together on building up and restoring our community to greatness.

PEOPLE: Along with our purpose, we pledge to be as creative as we can in leaving our communities more beautiful, more elegant, being good stewards of our gifts.

ALL: Having all faith in God, the "God of our weary years, and our silent tears," we believe in the capacity of our elders, our parents, our teachers, our leaders, in each other, to help us move on toward victory, as we work for justice and equality.

Vow of Commitment

On this glorious day, we recommit ourselves to honor the gift of unity as a foundational standard and practice that serves as the springboard for our community enrichment and honoring our ancestors and rich African legacy. We honor our productive and collective labor and aspire to be better stewards of our resources. Fitting our walk to embrace the seven principles of unity, self-determination, collective work and responsibility, cooperative economics, purpose, creativity, and faith we refocus on the importance of family, community, and culture. We look to God and deep within as we seek to discern what it means to be a human being of the African diaspora in a holistic, healthy sense.

Embracing the seven principles and seven related symbols of the crops, candle holder, mat, corn, candles, unity cup, and gifts, we commit to making family a priority: our biological, adoptive, extended, and church families are critical to us as relationships are the most important reality in our lives. We pledge to rethink our understanding of community, and in so doing will become good stewards of all of our resources—creativity, time, finances—that we grow individually and collectively. Given the phenomenal depth and wealth of our cultural legacy, we will honor our heritage and ourselves by engaging less in consumerism and participating more in the simple things of life; in appreciating art, music, literature, and the scientific accomplishments of black people. We will take time to read and learn more about our heritage, that we can better equip our children and young adults to understand the tremendous history that has gone before them. We come today to appreciate our heritage and ourselves. Blessed be.

Suggested Colors

Red, green, and black are the colors for Kwanzaa. Red stands for love, living blood, emotion, strife, ardor, passion, anger, and warmth. Green denotes steadiness, thoughtfulness, freshness, healing, peace, visibility, growth, and the divine. Black symbolizes solidarity, strength, power, infinity. That is, Dr. Karenga says, black for the people, red for their struggle, and green for the future and hope that comes from their struggle.

Scriptures

The earth has yielded its increase; God, our God, has blessed us. (Ps. 67:6)

Faithfully they brought in the contributions, the tithes and the dedicated things. (2 Chr. 31:12a)

If God so clothes the grass of the field, which is alive today and tomorrow is thrown into the oven, how much more will [God] clothe you—you of little faith! (Luke 12:28)

If the part of the dough offered as first fruits is holy, then the whole batch is holy; and if the root is holy, then the branches also are holy. (Rom. 11:16)

Poem of Reflection

KWANZAA: HONORING ANCESTORS AND OURSELVES

Looking back,
Realizing that we got over
Because of our ancestors, their faith in God,
And their creative tenacity to make
Quilts out of rags; haute cuisine out of scraps;
Hew fine gardens out of clay;
Weave majestic words out of their creative imaginations;
We got over as we lived in community.

We, the us-ness of ourselves
Helped to stabilize a world of chaos;
The misbegotten anguish of oppression
That called men "boys," and women "gals,"
That made disrespect holy;
That chose to dub us 3/5 a human
To allow other folks a chance to vote;
That denigrated our souls and skins
Yet, did not and will ultimately
Not triumph when we remember
Who we are and whose we are,
In unity, in community.

We are the children of Kwanzaa,
The firstfruits of God
Of them, from the mother continent
The land where people emerged
Back then, way back then;
And now,
we celebrate ourselves,
For we have gotten over some;
Lots to yet get over still
In unity, in faith,
With family and self-determination;
Working together, collectively, with purpose
Keeping our faith and living with integrity

Means we will become the village
That can raise the children
Who will be allergic to prison;
Who will hold on to God's hand;
Who will bless us still
Who will remember and become griots
Who proclaim the essential importance of
Family, Community, Culture:
Together we stand; together we can.

APPENDIX

Original *AFRICAN AMERICAN SPECIAL DAYS*
Copyright © 1996 by Cheryl A. Kirk-Duggan

1. Children and Youth Days
2. Sunday School Conventions and Youth Conferences
3. Graduation and Promotion Days
4. Homecoming and Family Reunions
5. Mother's Day
6. Father's Day
7. Women's Day
8. Men's Day
9. Pastor's Appreciation Day
10. Officers' Rededication Day
11. Board and Auxiliary Day
12. Groundbreaking, Cornerstone Laying, and Mortgage Burning
13. Church Building Dedication
14. Choir Anniversary Day
15. Black History Celebration